An essential, easy-reference guide to brilliant branding by corporate-identity guru **Wally Olins**

'World-class thought leader Wally Olins has done it again! In a compelling and clear argument he shows how everybody can learn to master branding'

– Professor Majken Schultz, Copenhagen Business School

Many people talk about branding, but very few people know how to actually do it. Wally Olins, generally recognized as the world's most experienced practitioner of corporate identity and branding, draws on a lifetime's experience to present a concise, practical guide. He explains – in trademark straightforward fashion – what brands are, how to create them, how to make them work, and how to sustain them. All aspects of the process are covered, from developing the 'core idea', creating the name and designing the logo to launching and managing a successful branding programme. Inspirational as well as practical, this easy-reference manual is essential reading for anyone interested in the field of corporate identity and branding.

WITHDRAWN

Wally Olins: The Brand Handbook

Thames & Hudson

Wally Olins: The Brand Handbook

with 120 illustrations, 93 in colour

First published in the United Kingdom in 2008
by Thames & Hudson Ltd, 181A High Holborn,
London WC1V 7QX

www.thamesandhudson.com

British Library Cataloguing-in-Publication Data
A catalogue record for this book is available
from the British Library

ISBN 978-0-500-51408-5

Printed and bound in China by Midas Printing
International Ltd

CONTENTS

Preface

Brands and branding are all-pervasive and ubiquitous. The media are obsessed with brands, and everybody now uses the 'brand' word.

In recent times enormous changes have taken place in the world of branding which have put it right in the spotlight. These changes include:
— the development of digital technology
— the emergence of the high-profile company
— branding moving from the periphery to the centre of corporate concern
— branding moving into countries, regions and cities, and also into charities, the arts and academia
— and perhaps above all the changing attitude of society to environmental dangers, and the beginning of the emergence of a more caring twenty-first-century society. This handbook reflects these new trends.

The book has been written based around the vast collective experience that my colleagues and I have had both at Saffron and in our former companies. The thoughts and methodologies outlined in the book derive largely from our current operational practice.

The book has a practical purpose. It is a guide to branding – what branding is and how it works. I've tried to keep it clear of jargon and unnecessary complexity. At the end of most of the sections there are suggested thoughts to take away.

The book is intended to help the people who look after brands do just that. It is also intended to help students of business, design and allied subjects get a real grip on the subject. Anybody who works for an organization, from the chairman onwards, is involved with its brand; anybody who lives in today's world is involved in branding. This handbook is for each of you.

Wally Olins
London
2008

A retail shopping area in Hong Kong. The plethora of brands, both local and global, all shout as loud as they can.

Introduction

A brand is simply an organization, or a product, or service with a personality. So why all the fuss?

Despite the ubiquity of brands and branding, and despite all the talk, surprisingly few people seem to understand what they are actually all about. The subject is confused and confusing. This is partly because branding can encapsulate both big and important and apparently superficial and trivial issues simultaneously.

Consumer products

For some people, brands are still just where they began – heavily advertised consumer products; groceries that you can buy, bring home and use, such as soap, washing powder and coffee, or more sophisticated goods like scent, suntan lotion and over-the-counter pills that ease indigestion and similar ailments.

Retail outlets

And yet, by some kind of osmosis, the stores and supermarkets in which these branded products are sold have also morphed into brands, and many people have very strong views about them. In Britain, for example, people view the Tesco brand and the Waitrose brand very differently. The Waitrose brand is generally admired, even cherished, while the Tesco brand – despite its extraordinary success in attracting customers – is unloved, even loathed.

However you view it, Wal-Mart is an astonishing achievement of consumer capitalism.

Wal-Mart in the US is both the most successful retailer in the world, which presumably means that some people like going there, and also the most violently disliked, not so much because of what it is, but what it represents: it kills small shops; kills city centres; pays its employees ('associates') badly; imports huge amounts from China and thereby destroys US jobs, and so on. For some people Wal-Mart represents branding at its most triumphalist, globalist, greedy and oppressive.

Luxury goods

For many people, brands seem to represent the most extravagant and wild excesses of a society in love with consumerism and display. In their view the most useless, vulgar, absurdly priced trash is made desirable only because it becomes a heavily promoted brand charged with all kinds of sexual and social innuendo. Brands, they say, represent the consumerist society at its sickest.

Spanish luxury accessories brand Trash and Soul both decries and celebrates the disposable society, with a twist of irony and humour, by elevating garbage into gold jewelry.

A squiggle

For other people, or perhaps for the same people at a different moment of the day, a brand is something else. It is a symbol, a logo, a squiggly design on a piece of paper, a website or a visiting card – or on something even more sizeable like the tailfin of an aircraft. This kind of branding, a few colours and a funny typeface,

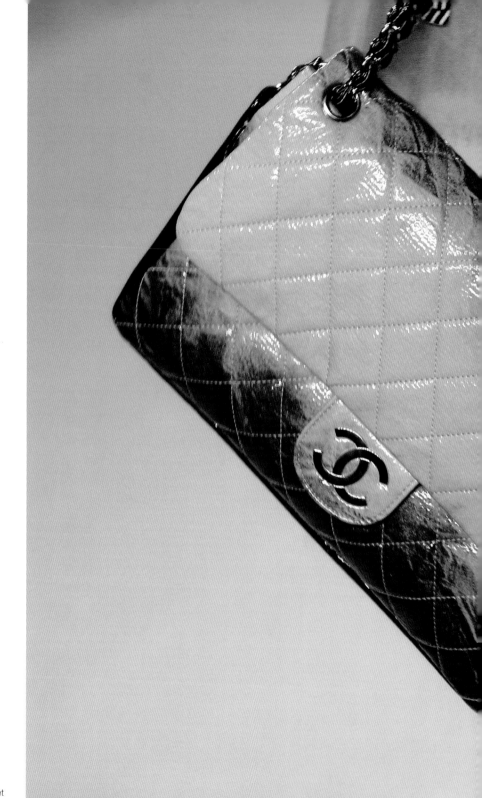

Chanel – the kind of bag to see and be seen with, but not to bring the supermarket shopping home in.

especially when it is newly introduced, is almost always regarded with suspicion, if not disdain. 'What kind of a fast one are they trying to pull this time? The only thing that has changed is the logo.'

Such branding activities are often contemptuously called 'makeovers'. These, it is thought, happen when nothing much is changing, but they (whoever they are) are pretending it has. Makeovers are regarded as an expensive waste of time and money, and are therefore frequent subjects of ridicule in the media. 'They've made it look different, but it's really the same. Who are they trying to kid?' Sometimes new squiggles provoke remarkable levels of contention. In the UK, the Olympic 2012 logo was the subject of several front-page, high-profile comments: surprising in a way, considering the controversy was over a piece of graphic design – a few lines and blocks on bits of paper and some stuff that jumped around on the screen.

The controversial London 2012 Olympic logo.

A big idea

On the other hand, there is a further aspect of brands and branding that is implicitly recognized but rarely explicitly referred to – which is that brands can represent a huge and complex idea. Groups of people with particular ways of life or attitudes – like the Sloane Ranger in Britain or the Blue Collar Worker and Redneck in the US – are branded. Even ideas like Intelligent Design are branded. Brands like these encapsulate great swathes of social and cultural behaviour, religious attitudes, socio-economic groupings and, of course, voting habits.

Sometimes rebranding also takes place as a sign that something new and different is happening. When the Czechs and Slovaks parted company in the Velvet Revolution of 1989, both countries adopted new flags and the other paraphernalia of statehoods as symbols of change. They rebranded themselves.

The logo of the UK Conservative party, before it went 'green', and after.

Style and substance

What it all boils down to is that, in branding, style is frequently confused with substance. In a way this is not so surprising, because it is the outward and visible signs of the brand that are the symbols of differentiation. That is why the Stars and Stripes is an object of veneration in the United States where it is regularly and proudly waved, while it is excoriated and regularly torched in the Middle East. The red, white and blue bunting, the symbol, is conflated with a perception of the country, about which people feel very strongly.

Advertising and product brands

For about a hundred years – till the dawn of the technological age – the world of communications was dominated by advertising and advertising agencies. The reason why advertising was so important was because until recently corporations believed that they only had one important audience to address – the final consumer, the person who bought their products. Advertising agencies provided the tools to meet this challenge. Manufacturers either used their corporate name, such as Heinz or Kellogg's, to brand their products, or increasingly they created special names – brand names – like Sunlight or Dove, which were intended to embody specific product characteristics and which enabled manufacturers to put a multiplicity of overlapping goods on the market. But the big companies behind these product brands stayed in the background. They may have had a corporate identity, but it was only promoted in a very limited way to a small and carefully selected audience. Advertising drove home the virtues of the individual product to the customer.

There wasn't very much media but what there was went everywhere. An advertiser could pick the target audience, launch a product in the press, on TV and the other media to get blanket coverage. The audience – that is, the customers – were divided into a few simple socio-economic groups, As, Bs, C1s, C2s, Ds and so on, and give or take a bit, provided the product worked OK, was competitively priced and readily available, they bought what they were offered.

Complex media

Those days now seem laughably simple. It just isn't like that anymore. The proliferation of media – the digital world, information technology, the web, blogs, the development of a complex, sophisticated, multi-faceted audience with individual quirks and behaviour patterns, the tremendous increase in purchasing power in the West and increasingly in Asia, the increasing homogeneity of competitive products and services, the increasing competition in every field of activity, the emergence of a caring society, but above all the requirement nowadays for corporations to come out

Some people in some places like the US flag; other people in other places don't.

Helios House in Los Angeles is designed to dramatize the identity of its owner BP as a new-age energy company. The restrained claim that this is merely 'a little better gas station' is made more than credible by the use of recycled materials, renewable wood and a rainwater-collecting canopy, among other amenities.

a little better.

good

better

best

gasoline

of the shadows and communicate with all of their audiences – have altered the balance of power and made the corporate brand central in twenty-first-century life. Corporations have left the business pages: their activities are now front-page news. Corporate behaviour in society affects recruitment, share price, acquisitions and every other aspect of corporate life. Today the corporation has become the brand – for all its audiences. So whether it owns multiple brands promoted quite separately from its corporate brands or whether it only has a corporate brand, the corporation has to promote itself – to all of its audiences.

The emergence of the corporate brand

It is becoming increasingly evident that the nature of competition is changing. It was once possible to choose between competing products and services on the basis of price, quality or service – rational or quasi-rational factors. Today in most activities that is no longer possible. Look at financial services, petrol retailing and parcel delivery services, just to take some broad industrial and commercial areas at random. In all of these activities there is very little or no real difference between the products and services of the leading players in terms of price, quality and service – the rational factors.

Being as good as the best of the competition is now sufficient only to enable an organization to stay in the race. In such situations, emotional factors – being liked, admired or respected more than the competition – help the organization to win. And that is why so many organizations now invest so heavily in what is increasingly being called 'corporate branding'. They want a complete and overlapping range of audiences – both internal and external – to respect and admire them. And that is why we now have a situation in which corporate brands exist side by side with product brands. As I explain later (see p. 44), organizations have a number of different models to choose from when they develop systems to control and modulate their own brands or to absorb new brands. These systems come under the term 'brand architecture'. But there is no doubt that the 'corporate brand' – that is, the organization using its corporate name to project the whole – is becoming increasingly important.

Aggressive driving, like speeding, braking hard and stomping down on the gas, can dramatically increase emissions and decrease your fuel economy. Drive happy.

A little less gas. A little more Zen.
thegreencurve.com

Recycle. Reduce waste. Smell the flowers.
Soak this handmade paper postcard in water overnight and plant under a thin layer of soil. Keep thoroughly moist until seedlings are well established. Seedlings will sprout in 1–4 weeks.
©2007 BP Products North America, Inc.
* Source: U.S. Department of Energy (fueleconomy.gov)

Cheery and informed dressed-down BP attendants distribute seed-impregnated leaflets (you can plant them), which read: 'Recycle. Reduce waste. Smell the flowers.'

The external/internal audience

Traditionally product brands – particularly fast-moving consumer goods in supermarkets – have been directed at an external audience. This was predominantly the customer – usually the housewife, the person who bought the stuff in the shop. That's why, historically, advertising has been so important.

But external audiences are becoming much more complex. Until relatively recently corporations did not feel any particular pressure to deal with their reputation amongst journalists, financial analysts, competitors, suppliers, national and local government, potential employees and all the other audiences with whom they come into contact, in any cohesive, structured fashion. Different audiences got different treatment at different times: some were totally ignored all the time, others were only addressed when there was a crisis. Now all that has changed. The corporate reputation is recognized as a very valuable resource which has to be managed from the centre in a coherent, sophisticated and long-term fashion.

Different audiences form a view of an organization based on the totality of the impressions that it makes on them. Where the impressions are contradictory – where impressions made in one place are different from those made somewhere else – the overall impression will be negative, or at any rate confusing. In a world which is increasingly transparent and open, it is no longer possible for the corporation to hide from anyone (even that least publicly accountable group of organizations that make up the private equity business have found that out).

In addition, over the past few decades, developments in service branding have meant that internal audiences – the organization's own people – have become much more important than ever before. This means that most companies have to operate major corporate branding programmes which are aimed at influencing all parts of the internal organization – design, marketing, sales, customer relations and service, purchasing, recruitment, finance and so on – and also influencing the external world – legislators, stockbrokers, analysts, journalists and all kinds of other opinion-formers – in a coherent, comprehensible fashion.

Increasingly of course companies also outsource. They outsource design, manufacture, security, human

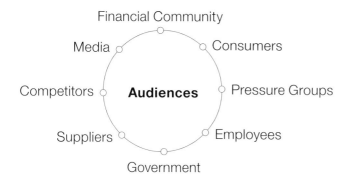

Financial Community

Media • Consumers

Competitors • **Audiences** • Pressure Groups

Suppliers • Employees

Government

resources: in fact quite often it's difficult to know where the borders between the company and its partners (they used to be called 'suppliers') lies. These partners/suppliers have to feel part of the corporate family too.

In addition to all this, the pressure on companies to behave responsibly to society and to demonstrate this commitment publicly and continuously is growing rapidly. This change in the social scene and climate is having a vast impact on the way companies behave, or seem to behave, and how they communicate about their role in society.

The capability to encompass both internal and external worlds can be a source of strength, because it brings with it cohesion, coherence and clarity.

Brand value

Today it is of course commonplace for corporations, and the divisions and subsidiaries which control the brands they own and manage, to operate sophisticated branding programmes. Every large enterprise with a brand, or brands, attempts to guard them with extreme care. Brands now appear regularly on balance sheets in many companies. The intangible value of the brand is often much greater than the corporation's tangible assets. Look at McDonald's, Diageo, Nestlé or Danone. But it's still very difficult for some people, including many of those who purport to look after them, to know what a brand actually is, let alone how to value it.

Managing the brand asset

There is little indication that the majority of the people within an organization understand how their brands work, where a brand begins and ends, or why perceptions of their corporate and product brands

Now commonplace are journals, conferences, consultancies and professional associations dedicated to the idea – in many ways mistaken – that brands can be managed like financial assets.

Frank Gehry
– something of a brand
himself – is helping turn
Guggenheim into a
franchised brand.

The Manchester United
soccer club has retail
stores in places as far
flung from northwest
England as Singapore.

change. Even though many chairmen and CEOs have a sense that the corporate reputation affects recruitment, acquisitions, sales, collaborative agreements, relationships with other stakeholders and share price, they still don't know how to place a value on their brand or how to manage and control it. However, because brands are now understood to be assets valuable to any organization, it is clearly mandatory to husband them with extreme care – even though the truth is that very few people know how.

Branding beyond commerce

Branding has of course moved way beyond the commercial area. We live in a world in which opera companies, orchestras, charities, universities, film companies and sports clubs are also brands. Guggenheim in the arts and Manchester United in soccer are genuine global brands. In addition, in an increasingly globalizing and in some ways also fragmented era, cities, regions and nations are developing full-scale branding programmes, partly to encourage self-confidence and self-esteem and their own sense of place, and partly to attract inward investment and tourism. So what with one thing and another, branding is a lot bigger, more high-profile and more complex a subject than appears at first sight. Brands and branding are a vast, growing, confused and confusing area. That is why this handbook exists.

Identity in the twenty-first century

Identity in its various manifestations has grabbed our hearts and minds, because we are desperate to express our need to belong but also overtly to differentiate ourselves and our aspirations from those around us. If identity is the idea that marks the twenty-first century, then branding operates at its point of delivery. With all this interest, how can it be that only a very few people can even say what a brand really is, let alone know how to create one, introduce it, manage it and sustain it?

Why does the Red Cross collect far more than any other aid organization whenever disaster strikes? Because it's the leading brand in the charity field.

Lloyd's needs to remain different

Familiarity can dull perception; so, for all of us whose working lives revolve around Lloyd's, it's important to remind ourselves just how different this extraordinary insurance market actually is. And, given that Lloyd's success is built upon that difference, it's even more important that we maintain it.

But that's going to be a challenge. Because in a world where regulation and globalisation increasingly rule, the pressure on Lloyd's is to conform; to become more "corporate"; to bring our business practices into line with industry standards.

To a large extent, we have no choice about this; even Lloyd's can't swim against the tide. So this is where our **constant originality** is going to be tested: in finding ways of responding to the pressure on us to become more similar to our competitors, while remaining as different as possible from them.

And make no mistake, it's essential that we do so if we want to continue to attract more good quality specialist insurance business and the best talent.

Constant originality: since 1688
Of course, the way Lloyd's does business today bears little resemblance to the coffee shop opened by Edward Lloyd. Yet it would be impossible to exaggerate the extent to which our history has moulded Lloyd's. From our complex market structure to the trust which the Lloyd's name inspires around the world, our unique present bears the imprint of our unparalleled past.

Striking a balance, keeping our edge

That means, for example, that as well as applying strict discipline to our underwriting, we must continue to give our expert underwriters the freedom to make quick decisions, and to back their judgement.

It means that, while the market needs to act in a commercially disciplined way, Lloyd's must also continue to be prepared to write new risks. Our legendary appetite for risk must never be dulled.

And it means that, while we have every reason to be proud of our history and heritage, we should never wallow in it. If there's a new and better way of doing things, Lloyd's should be the first to adopt it.

As we said, this isn't going to be easy. Because what we're talking about is a tightrope act: a perpetual need to find a balance between what has to change and what we want to preserve.

But we must succeed. Because there is a huge amount at stake here: nothing less, we believe, than Lloyd's ability to remain the world's leading specialist insurance market for another three centuries.

Constant originality: making things happen
The world be a very different place without Lloyd's. Because, without the creative thinking of our underwriters, many things which take place simply wouldn't be able to happen. The Olympics are a case in point; a bewilderingly complex accumulation of different types of risk, from potential injuries to athletes to the threat of terrorism. Leave it to Lloyd's, and let the Games begin!

Once again, if you accept the basic premise of this booklet – that the most successful businesses are built around an idea understood and shared by all within the organisation – that question should answer itself.

You are responsible for bringing our brand idea to life, by ensuring that it is reflected in everything you say and do during the working day.

Of course, how you do this will depend on where you fit into the Lloyd's community. An underwriter's **constant originality** will manifest itself very differently from an IT specialist's or even a security guard's. But we all have a part to play – especially in relation to Lloyd's customers.

WHAT'S THE BIG IDEA?

Brand books – like this one for the legendary insurance market Lloyd's – help people grasp the essentials of what a company means and stands for.

Definitions in branding

Like almost everything to do with the world of branding, the terminology is in a state of flux. Until the 1980s or so a 'brand' was a fast-moving consumer product on a supermarket shelf. It essentially appealed to only one audience of the organization, the customer.

When the corporation presented itself to all of its audiences, the phrase 'corporate identity' was used. Many years ago in *The Corporate Personality* (Design Council, 1978) I wrote that 'corporate personality' is the soul, the persona, the spirit of the organization manifested in some comprehensible way. I then wrote: 'The tangible manifestation of a corporate personality is its corporate identity.' This latter, then, was the corporate personality under cultivation.

Today, however, one would probably say that the tangible manifestation of corporate personality is called the 'corporate brand'. Although the term 'corporate identity' is fighting a tough rearguard battle, 'corporate brand' is winning. The word 'brand' can therefore embrace both the corporation as a whole and its products and its services. The word 'brand' also has more financially accountable connotations than those terms it is gradually supplementing or replacing, like 'identity', 'image' and 'reputation'.

The 'corporate image' is what all the audiences of the corporation perceive of the identity that has been created and projected.

Guidelines for branding

Branding has now become a significant mainstream management activity. It can be, although it isn't always, a complex, multi-faceted and multi-disciplinary process. It can be consecutively – or, more frequently, simultaneously – a marketing resource, a design resource, a communications resource and a behavioural resource. All this makes it pretty difficult to pin down, but branding activity is generally associated with a few simple rules. These are that branding

— is a design, marketing, communication and human resources tool

— should influence every part of the organization and every audience of the organization all the time

— is a co-ordinating resource because it makes the corporation's activities coherent

— above all makes the strategy of the organization visible and palpable for all audiences to see.

'Idents', as we call them in the trade, often come in families, where individuals do their own thing but all look a little (or a lot) alike. Here BBC Radio branding shows the coherence of the corporation's activities.

PART ONE

What Branding is About

People, at least in the
West, have become
extremely brand fluent.
Some brands we know
so well they don't even
have to tell us who
they are.

Section 1 – Brand Visibility

Looked at from the outside, the brand seems to consist of a few elements – some colours, some typefaces, a strapline or slogan, all topped off with a logo or symbol, sometimes of an apparently allegorical nature but frequently consisting of a simple typeface. Sometimes a brand also embraces sound or music, and even smells. All of these ingredients seem to be mixed up and then plastered apparently more or less at random over everything that the organization owns or influences.

In real life, though, it's a bit more complicated than that. Every organization of a substantial size carries out hundreds of thousands of transactions every day. It sells to distributors, dealers and the final consumer. It outsources design and manufacture and other very important parts of its business to companies who may be thousands of miles away, operating in different time zones with their own traditions and ambitions. It hires or works with people who perhaps come from a multiplicity of social, economic, national, religious and ethnic backgrounds, and who therefore have varied cultural patterns. It markets its products through a chain of third-party dealers and distributors all over the world. It deals with local governments and central governments. It also has relationships with stakeholders of different kinds, including investors, financial journalists and other commentators. And increasingly the organization, especially if it's a commercial enterprise, is becoming much more high-profile than ever before. It is seen as an entity and scrutinized by society, often critically.

In all its transactions, the organization will in some way be presenting itself – or part of itself – to some or all of the groups of people with whom it has relationships. If it is to be successful in holding all these disparate groups together, it has to be consistent and clear in what it says and does in all these relationships. In other words, if it is to be seen as an entity, it must behave as an entity, and the corporate brand it projects to all of its audiences must be consistent.

All organizations have a brand or corporate image whether they especially manage it or not and whether they are aware of it or not. Of course when the organization is very small – one or even a few shops or offices, say – it is possible to manage it in an informal, implicit way. But when it becomes bigger, the range of activity becomes so vast and the manifestations of the brand so complex, that it all has to be managed explicitly. This is the point at which branding becomes a significant, mainstream management activity.

Branding embraces and is associated with marketing, design, internal and external communication and human resources. It becomes the channel through which the organization presents itself to itself and to its various external worlds. It influences every part of the organization and every audience of the organization – all the time, everywhere.

Wherever a brand has a 'touchpoint' – that is, an interaction with an audience – it needs to look, feel or behave like itself.

Brand Visibility

Section 1

Part One

Sometimes brands
seem to be like rats
pressing the lever
to get food pellets
– feverishly and
apparently mindlessly
splashing their logos
on anything that moves.

The core idea

The fundamental idea behind the brand is that in everything the organization does, everything it owns, and everything it produces it should project a clear idea of what it is and what its aims are. The most significant way in which this can be done is by making everything in and around the organization – its products, environment, communication and behaviour – consistent in purpose and performance and, where this is appropriate, in appearance too.

Outward consistency of this kind will only be achieved, and for that matter is only appropriate, if it is the manifestation of an inward consistency – a consistency of purpose. This consistency of purpose derives from the vision, or the core idea, and is almost always the base from which a successful branding programme can be developed.

The core idea drives the organization. It is what the organization is about, what it stands for, what it believes in. All organizations are unique even if the products/services they make/sell are more or less the same as those of their competitors. It is the company's history, structure, strategy, the personalities who have created and driven it forward, its successes and its failures, that shape it and make it what it is.

Most organizations are not naturally especially conscious or thoughtful about these matters. If they have a core idea it is implicitly enshrined in the way they get on with their business. The company's behaviour patterns, its communications and the appearance of its products, services, offices and showrooms are usually the result of the unconscious influence of a few powerful individuals, quite often working semi-independently. Companies grow up dominated more often than not by the personality of their founder. That is why what they look like and how they behave sometimes seems haphazard and unmanaged.

There always comes a time, however, in a successful organization when the informal, intuitive, perhaps muddled, but shared vision or core idea has to be uncovered or rediscovered; when it has to be recreated, formalized, clarified and made coherent. And that is when the explicit, institutionalized, self-aware branding programme is introduced. The corporate brand makes the organization's core idea and strategy visible and tangible.

Through a combination of design, celebrity backing and a compelling story, the American Express brand RED is trying to reintroduce the idea of tithing into twenty-first-century consumption habits.

Products

Behaviour ———— Core Idea ————→ Environment

Communication

The four vectors through which a brand emerges.

Lille, France

Australia

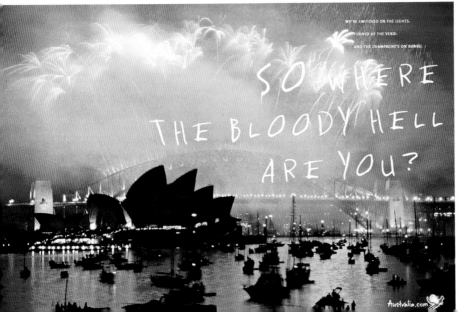

A distinctive personality shines through in these brand elements from Lille (European Capital of Culture 2004) and Australia.

Example

Mondragón, the world's largest industrial cooperative, emerged in Spain's Basque region in the 1950s to help lift craft workers out of poverty. Today the organization is huge but it remains true to its roots and corporate social responsibility runs deep in its culture. The phrase 'humanity at work' was developed by Saffron as the core idea that drives all member companies.

Take away

– Does your organization have a clear core idea?
– Can you explain what your company does and what makes it different from its competitors in a couple of sentences?
– Do most of your colleagues in the company share similar feelings about what the organization is, what it does and how it does it?
– Does the outside world understand what your company stands for, and how it differs from its competitors?

The visual elements

The prime identifier for almost all brands is the symbol or logo. The other tangible elements – colours, typefaces, straplines or slogans, tone of voice and style of expression (sometimes called 'look and feel') – are also very important, and collectively form the visible recognition pattern. But the central element of that visible recognition pattern is the logo itself. This usually lies at the heart of a branding programme. Its prime purpose is to present the core idea of the organization with impact, brevity and immediacy. The logo encapsulates the brand.

Symbols are immensely powerful. They act as visual triggers which work many times faster and more explosively than words to set ideas in the mind. Many symbols are, as we know from Jung and others, an intrinsic part of the human vocabulary of expression and comprehension. Symbols can unleash the most complex and profound emotions. When the communist regimes of Eastern Europe tottered and fell in the late 1980s, the first symbolic action the liberated peoples of each country took was publicly to topple the statues of Lenin and Stalin and cut out with scissors and knives the hammer and sickle from their national flags.

Take away

– Does your organization have an effective set of visual elements?
– Do the visual elements work according to a well understood and coherent system?
– Do they present an immediate memorable and unique encapsulation of the brand idea?
– If your organization is large, does each company, each division and each brand understand the workings of the organization's visual elements as a whole?

Logotype

Symbol

JUST DO IT.

Tagline

Exact definitions are elusive, but you won't go wrong if you regard a logotype as a word designed a particular way, a symbol as a strictly visual device and a tagline as the slogan of a brand.

The four vectors of brand tangibility

Together, the core idea and the visual elements mark out the brand territory. But to be really effective you have to be able to sense the brand. You may even be able to touch it and feel it so that it manifests the core idea. Perhaps the clearest way to understand how the brand makes itself tangible is to look at it through the four vectors through which it manifests itself. These are product, environment, communication and behaviour. They are the brand's four senses.

PRODUCT – what the organization makes and sells
ENVIRONMENT – the physical environment of the brand, how it lays out its stall
COMMUNICATION – how it tells people, every audience, about itself and what it's doing
BEHAVIOUR – how its people behave to each other and to the world outside.

The significance of each of these four vectors varies according to the marketplace in which the brand performs. Sometimes each vector is of equal

Brand Visibility

Section 1

Yes, cars are sold in
fancy showrooms,
advertised abundantly
with clever, stylish
ads, and sold with
all manner of service
and warranty options.
Yet at its heart the
automobile – even the
personality-driven MINI
from BMW – remains
a product-dominated
brand.

Part One

significance in contributing to the overall brand personality. Sometimes one or two dominate.

Just to take a few examples: in the world of financial services there isn't usually much difference between products. They tend to be similar, even identical, so the other vectors emphasize differentiation: where products are sold – that is, environments; how they are promoted – that is, communications; and how the people who work for the organization behave. These things vary greatly between organizations and enable us to compare one brand with another. In financial services, the three most important vectors are normally environment, communication and behaviour (where a financial services brand is sold online, there may be no environment – so what matters most in that situation will be communication and behaviour).

In restaurants, however, all four vectors of branding are closely intertwined. Of course we judge a restaurant partly by its product. If the food is overpriced, dull or just not very good we won't go there again. But the environment, the experience of being in the place, is also very important. If we find it attractive, comfortable, stylish, well designed or quirky, it strongly affects us. If the service – that is, behaviour – is attentive and friendly, that matters too. Conversely, however good the food and attractive the environment, if the service is over-fussy or inattentive or overbearing we hate that as well. Finally there's communication; we have to know about the place. The restaurant might derive strength from word-of-mouth communication; if it's fashionable, people talk about it. So in restaurants all four vectors are mixed up.

Perhaps the classic example of a brand in which all four vectors are more or less equal and totally intertwined is a theme park. In Walt Disney World or Disneyland the four vectors of branding are so inextricably linked that it's almost impossible to tell where one begins and the other ends.

In our minds, a pepper bought at a farmers' market tastes better than the same one sold in shrink wrap at the 7-Eleven on the corner.

Product – what the organization makes and sells

In companies that design, make and sell things, the product is almost always the base from which the brand is defined and from which it emerges with the most clarity.

A classic example might be Apple. Apple products are designed to look beautiful and to function well:

The Hofbräuhaus
in Munich is a place
people go for the
atmosphere and
raucousness more
than for the Weissbier.

Brand Visibility

Section 1

Part One

The Magic Kingdom
and its Disney brethren,
first envisioned more
than half a century ago,
are arguably the
ultimate branded
environments.

The Madinat Jumeirah
in Dubai, dating all
the way from 2003,
presents itself as an
ancient Arabian citadel,
with an imitation
souk that rivals the
real thing. A thrilling,
well-wrought theme
park of Arabiana,
this environmentally
dominated brand has
enough correct details
to create an authentic
sense of place.

in doing that they project the Apple brand idea. So every Apple product helps both to define and to reinforce the brand. If Apple ever made a product that didn't look and work as we have come to expect, we would recognize it at once: 'This isn't an Apple, it's a lemon,' we might say.

Although everything, from the instruction literature, to the website, to the advertising, to the stores and the behaviour of the people who work in them, all help to support and sustain the Apple brand, the prime vector through which we perceive the Apple brand is the Apple product. When you hold an iPod, you have in your hand the essence of Apple. That is why we can call Apple a product-led brand – and there are plenty more like that. Dyson, Bang & Olufsen, BlackBerry and of course all the car companies have product-led brands.

There isn't that much difference in price or performance between, let's say, a similar class of Volvo and Alfa Romeo, but there's an immense difference in the way they look and the way they handle, the noise they make, even the way the doors open and shut. There's also a big difference in the way people feel about them. It's the product that primarily conveys the brand idea. Communication, environment and behaviour, especially sales and service behaviour, are all key factors in product-led branding, but if the product isn't right you can forget the rest.

Environment – the physical environment of the brand, how it lays out its stall

Environmental factors in branding are increasingly being called brand experiences. There isn't anything new about this. All food markets everywhere are environmentally led. They are fun to walk around. Go to a fish market in a port early in the morning. It's a joyful experience.

Exactly the same factors apply in department stores. They're usually nice places to be in. You can walk around them, jostle with and stare at other customers, have a coffee or a snack, handle the merchandise and buy if you feel like it. You don't have to rush. That's why so many department stores are environmentally led brands.

Supermarkets, despite resistance from their financial people with their focus on sales per square metre, are also moving in this direction.

For a mere few hundred dollars a night, you can follow in the footsteps of Ottoman sultans at the Ciragan Palace Hotel Kempinski Istanbul – another environmentally led brand, but what an environment.

Most hotels are, too. We choose hotels (apart from the price) because of what it feels like to be in them, what facilities they have and where they are located. All these are environmental factors. Some people unconsciously, or at least subconsciously, choose predictable environments. Most Holiday Inns are intended to be pretty much the same, which is why a lot of people choose to stay in them. But many people also look for special and particular environments. All the new, small, minimalist smart hotels featured in 'Hip Hotels' guides are environmentally led.

My favourite hotel, the Ciragan Palace in Istanbul, doesn't have the best food or service of any hotel I know but it does have the most extraordinary site and an overwhelming environment. Well it should: it was designed as an Ottoman palace and put down on the shores of the Bosphorus on the edge of Europe and Asia. In hotels it's the environment that leads the brand. Of course, communication, behaviour and product matter. Nobody would go to a hotel twice, however beautifully designed, furnished and located, if the food and service were lousy. But it is the environment that sets the tone.

Communication – how the organization talks about itself and to itself

There are some organizations in which the communications process is the prime means by which the identity emerges. Coca-Cola, like many fast-moving consumer brands, has an identity largely created and consistently fostered through promotion and advertising on an immense scale over more than a hundred years. That's why people say that Coke has a powerful brand image. There is nothing particularly special about the product that separates Coca-Cola from other similar drinks: it's just a maroon, fizzy, sweetish drink that is momentarily refreshing. There are plenty of other drinks that do the same job. So why is Coke one of the world's best known and loved products? Because of consistent, ubiquitous distribution and promotion. Wherever you go there's Coke – and they're not kidding. Coke is not just about advertising, of course. Coke tries to become, and often succeeds in becoming, part of the consumer's lifestyle.

To take a more extreme example of drinks brands that are communication-led, look at bottled water. Why is bottled water so fashionable? Water is, we are told, very good for us. We should drink lots of it. But why does it have to be imported into, say, Japan from France, Italy or the Highlands of Scotland? Does this kind of water taste so very different from local water out of a tap? Not really. Some people claim they can tell the difference. But after just one gulp? Doubtful. Even if it has bubbles they're often added by machine. But bottled water has emotional connotations of health, purity, activity and fitness which seem to have a special resonance. And very many people, including me, are perfectly prepared to pay relatively large sums of money for the emotional satisfaction they derive from drinking it. It's primarily communication that makes Badoit, Perrier and the rest so successful.

But communication has another aspect, too. The internet has made communication even more significant than ever before. And it has also changed its nature. Until a few years ago communication was a one-way street, the brand or the company to the customer. Now the customer can communicate with the company – and just as important, the customer can communicate with other customers all over the world about the company and its brands. If customers don't like the brand they can tell the world via blogs.

All this has changed the rules. Corporate and brand communications have to be more sophisticated, more focussed and more varied, and maybe a bit less crass than before. Also, and this is becoming increasingly important, companies have to listen, as their customers become increasingly talkative, articulate and critical. What all this boils down to is that communication has become a more complex manifestation of the brand than ever before, and it has to be handled with considerable subtlety.

Behaviour – how the organization deals with its own people, and how they deal with the outside world

Every kind of service that we buy is behaviourally driven or influenced. Supermarkets and other retailers have a large behavioural element; so do airlines and financial services and hotels of course. There's hardly any organization that we come into contact with, from health to communication to transport to holidays to business or academic institutions, that doesn't involve a massive behavioural content, usually associated with one or more of the traditional brand elements.

Water, water everywhere, nor any drop unbranded. Bottled water represents the ultimate communication-led brand area: the triumph of the emotional over the rational in branding.

US Post Office

Singapore Airlines

'Post office girl, you're a great way to mail'? Let's face it, some organizations offer better service than others. But only the best, like Singapore Airlines, stake their brand on it. Both of the above are behaviourally dominated brands.

Hospitals are a very interesting mix. Product clearly matters: we wouldn't want to go to a hospital where the surgeons had a record of disaster. But our reactions to a hospital are largely based around environment and behaviour. It's what our ward or room looks like and how the nurses and doctors behave that we tend to make judgments on.

Airlines are also a classic example of behaviourally led brands. We almost always judge an airline on the basis of the service we received; not how long it took to go from Budapest to Amsterdam but what the experience was like from the moment we arrived at the airport till the time when we picked up our luggage – or didn't!

Behaviour is almost always the most significant element in service brands. Service-led branding is quite different from product-led branding. In a product brand, the customer experience, generally, is consistent. One Mars bar tastes much like another: however many times you eat it, it tastes the same. In a service brand, however, like an airline, every single experience is different – because every time you deal with different people. Ice cream doesn't get headaches or have trouble with kids, but the people who represent a service brand do.

In a service brand the people who work for the organization *are* the brand. They feel different at different times of the day. They get harassed, fed up and have worries. Product brands don't. And that's why service brands are much harder to manage than product brands. Because in a service brand you have to manage people.

The implication of this, of course, is that the service-based organization has to focus on its internal audience to a far greater extent than product-based organizations. That's why the phrase 'living the brand' is so appropriate for service businesses.

It is true that many traditional product brands are also service brands. You couldn't find a more technologically sophisticated product brand than a jet engine. But Rolls Royce, Pratt & Whitney and GE jet engines compete just as much on service issues – getting spares to the right place, servicing intervals, responding fast globally, going the extra mile to be really helpful – as they do on product issues such as technical specifications.

If your organization is primarily service-led, however, you have to invest sufficiently and consistently in staff training. Your staff – more than any others – need to live the brand and understand the relationship between service and product.

Take away

- What is the appropriate balance between the four vectors in your organization?
- Do you manage the interaction and interrelationship between the four vectors effectively?
- Do you have an appropriate management structure to deal with problems deriving from each of the vectors?

In some fields, like commercial jet engines, after-sales service is the primary brand differentiator.

Section 2 – Brand Architecture

Every organization needs to create a framework into which its brands fall. This is called 'brand architecture'. The architecture should be clear, easy to comprehend and consistent. The brand architecture of most organizations that have given consideration to the matter falls broadly into one of three categories.

CORPORATE, OR MONOLITHIC — THE SINGLE BUSINESS IDENTITY

The organization uses one name and one visual system throughout (e.g. Yamaha, Virgin, HSBC, Easy).

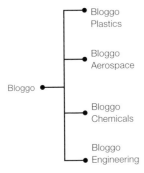

Bloggo

- Bloggo Plastics
- Bloggo Aerospace
- Bloggo Chemicals
- Bloggo Engineering

ENDORSED — THE MULTIPLE BUSINESS IDENTITY

The organization owns a variety of brands, each of which is endorsed by the group name or visual style (e.g. Nestlé, United Technologies, Banco Santander).

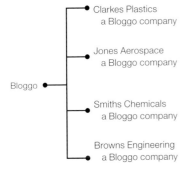

Bloggo

- Clarkes Plastics
  a Bloggo company
- Jones Aerospace
  a Bloggo company
- Smiths Chemicals
  a Bloggo company
- Browns Engineering
  a Bloggo company

BRANDED — THE BRAND-BASED IDENTITY

The organization owns a number of brands or companies which are apparently unrelated, both to each other and to the corporation (e.g. Diageo, Procter & Gamble, RBS [The Royal Bank of Scotland], General Motors).

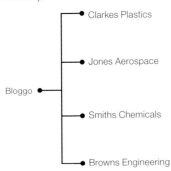

Bloggo

- Clarkes Plastics
- Jones Aerospace
- Smiths Chemicals
- Browns Engineering

Branding manages to make sense of some otherwise odd relationships. The motorcycle and the piano are both Yamaha products. Remember, Nokia used to make tyres.

These three categories are of course not mutually exclusive and rigidly defined. There is a great deal of overlap between them. Sometimes they exist because of sensible business logic. In other sectors there are venerable traditions, e.g. consumer goods companies tend to use the branded model, while oil companies traditionally use the corporate brand – although there are exceptions.

Corporate, or monolithic – the single business identity

Here the corporation is the brand: that's why it's called the corporate brand model. The overwhelming difference between the corporate brand model and the other two is that the corporate brand addresses every constituency of the organization – internal and external – while the other two models usually address only some audiences.

As I have pointed out earlier (see p. 15), because corporate behaviour is more visible than ever before, there is an increasing tendency for corporations to present themselves as a whole. That's why the corporate, or monolithic, model is becoming more fashionable.

In Japan and Korea there is a tradition of using the corporate name over a wide variety of activities, even where the companies using the same name are only loosely knit together. For example, Mitsubishi is a car, a bank, canned fish and many other things. Companies operating the corporate model quite deliberately use their corporate name to promote a particular idea about themselves.

Examples

Virgin is a striking example of an organization that uses a corporate brand system to best advantage. Its name and identity, stemming from the original music business, now embraces amongst other things an airline, a railway, financial services, a mobile phone business and a media business. When a product or service carries the Virgin name, it stands for a relaxed, informal, jaunty, friendly style. For many people evidently Virgin is not only a seal of a certain kind of quality, but a symbol of a way of life.

Kingfisher in India is both an airline and a beer brand … till now, but who knows how far the brand will be extended.

Kingfisher uses a monolithic brand architecture. Everything from a domestic Indian airline to an exported beer is similarly identified.

Harvard University is another example of an institution that uses a corporate brand system. Within Harvard there is a variety of different institutions, mostly called 'Harvard something': there is Harvard Business School, perhaps the world's best-known management school, which itself has further offshoots, such as Harvard Business School Press and Harvard Business Review magazine. Both of these derive strength from and add lustre to Harvard University as an entity.

Harvard University employs a more sophisticated monolithic identity, as seen in its university shield, B-School emblem and logo for the B-School's publishing house.

— The fundamental strength of the corporate or monolithic brand is that because each product and service launched by the organization has the same name, style and character as all the others, everything within the organization by way of promotion or product supports everything else. Because every audience sees the whole entity, relations with staff, suppliers and the outside world are clear, consistent, relatively easy to control and usually economical to manage.

— Companies with corporate brands tend as a consequence to have high visibility and a clear positioning, which can be a great advantage in the marketplace.

— The disadvantage, of course, is that if one bit of the business gets into trouble, it can affect everything else.

Endorsed – the multiple business identity

This is perhaps the most significant category, at least numerically. Many companies that have grown primarily by acquisition seek to employ the endorsed identity system because they hope to keep the best of both worlds. They can retain brands which may have cost them a lot of money and still have equity in the market place, and they can link their own names to them which gives the corporation more exposure. The endorsing organization is focussed on financial audiences, shareholders, commentators, governments, legislators, its own staff, potential staff, pensioners and similar groups, while the individual brands are usually focussed on customers and quite often the supply chain.

Example

A classic example of an endorsed model is United Technologies Corporation (UTC), which grew by acquiring very well known industrial companies. Otis

Whether for hotels or Spanish credit cards, endorsement tells you who owns the business.

Elevators and Sikorsky Helicopters, both part of UTC, are among the greatest names in their respective fields. UTC gives these and the other names in their industrial portfolio precedence with customers and suppliers, but it emphasizes the corporate United Technologies name with the stock market and certain other audiences. One of the major issues for UTC and companies like it is loyalty. Do people work for the division (Sikorsky, Hamilton, Otis) or for the whole corporation (UTC)? Quite often, while the front office has several brands, in the back office the proprietor corporation takes over. So loyalty may depend partly on which part of the organization you happen to work in. Of course it is true that it's possible for one individual to have a multiplicity of overlapping loyalties, so this may not be as big an issue as some people suggest.

The endorsed branding system is to be seen at its clearest in the military. All the various arms – infantry, armour, artillery, engineers, logistics and so on – have their own identities, brands to which they cling with loyalty bordering on fanaticism (try merging two Scottish Highland regiments for reasons of efficiency and see what reaction you get from veterans). In addition there is another, complementary structure – army corps, divisions, brigades and so on – formed from a complex mix of arms. This – at first sight, bewildering – collection of names, identities and traditions collectively forms the army, to which all serving soldiers regardless of their unit have an overriding loyalty. It seems very complicated but, once you understand it, it's very easy. Every military organization in the world uses it in some form. It's a system that works.

Organizations using an endorsed branding system normally have the following characteristics:
— They have grown largely by acquisition. They have often acquired competitors, suppliers and customers, each with its own name, culture, tradition and reputation amongst its own network of audiences.
— They are frequently multi-sector businesses, operating in a wide band of activities – manufacturing, wholesaling, retailing, selling components to competitors, making finished products themselves, and so on.
— They have sometimes acquired competitive ranges of products. They therefore have problems of

The militaries of all
nations are masters
of symbolism,
iconography and
– though they'd never
call it that – branding.

competition, even confusion, among suppliers, customers and often their own employees.
— They are concerned to retain the goodwill associated with the brands and companies which they have acquired, but at the same time they want to superimpose their own management style, reward systems, attitudes and sometimes name upon their subsidiaries.
— They have certain audiences, such as the financial world, opinion formers, possibly some suppliers and customers and so on, whom they want to impress with their total size and strength. Among these they want to emphasize coherence and consistency as opposed to heterogeneity.
— They frequently operate in many different countries, in which their product ranges and reputations may vary.

Companies seeking to create an identity covering a wide range of activities, with subsidiaries that have differing and frequently competitive backgrounds, face a complicated task. On the one hand, certainly at corporate level and for corporate audiences, they want to create a clear idea of a single but multi-faceted organization with a sense of purpose. On the other hand, they want to allow the identities of the numerous companies and brands they have acquired to continue to flourish in order to retain goodwill, both in the marketplace and among employees. These aims can only be achieved simultaneously, with the greatest possible sensitivity.

Branded – the brand-based identity

Some companies – for the most part those in pharmaceuticals, food, drink and other fast-moving consumer goods and fashion worlds – sometimes separate their identities as corporations from those of the brands which they market (e.g. Inditex, LVMH, GlaxoSmithKline, Pfizer). At the corporate level these companies reach out to all of the audiences of the corporate or endorsed branded company, except the final consumers. However, so far as the final customers are concerned the corporation does not exist. They are interested only in the brand.

Example

Diageo owns Guinness, Johnnie Walker and fifty or so other very famous brands, but nobody goes into a bar and orders a glass of Diageo. There's no confusion between Diageo and Guinness. What the customer perceives is only the individual brand.

The reasons why some companies pursue this policy are:

— Brands, it is thought, should be free to develop powerful identities of their own, appropriate to their consumers.
— The long-standing tradition of the fast-moving consumer goods industry is that the consumer is readily influenced by basic and obvious symbolism (e.g. Wash'n'Go = clean, fast and youthful, Poison = sophisticated, Flora = healthy). This somewhat naïve symbolism might seem to be inappropriate for a global, complex corporation.
— Brands may have a life-cycle of their own, quite distinct from that of the company.
— Brands from the same company may well compete in the marketplace and their integrity might appear to be damaged in the eyes of the consumer if they were known to come from the same stable, e.g. Louis Vuitton and Loewe.

DIAGEO

As a customer, you'll have to read the fine print to discover that all the above brands are owned by Diageo. But as an investment analyst or drinks distributor, you'll know it. And that's (partly) the point.

Modulation and modification: creating a brand identity

These three options outline the broad principles that brand architecture follows, but of course in real life there are a multitude of subtle variations which can be adapted to suit the corporate purpose. A rule to remember is that, everything being equal (which it isn't usually), the fewer brands you have the better.

Sometimes two organizations in the same business choose two completely different brand architecture models and it's difficult to determine why they've done it and which is the better route to follow.

Example

HSBC, formerly known as The Hong Kong and Shanghai Banking Corporation, with a few minor exceptions uses one name wherever it goes. It has created a high-profile corporate brand on a global basis. The core idea is to be the world's local bank. To do this it believes it needs one name that will enable it to challenge the leading global brand, Citi. It has taken over and eliminated banking names like Midland in the UK, The British Bank of the Middle East, CCF in France and so on, each with a massive local

HSBC is HSBC
everywhere (almost).

The Royal Bank of
Scotland lets its
constituent brands
fly free.

tradition, in some cases with reputations going back over a century – all in favour of HSBC. The monolithic or corporate brand model has served HSBC well. It is one of the most famous banking names in the world and it is hugely successful. In the same financial services sector, Royal Bank of Scotland is also a monumentally successful institution, but it has a completely different brand architecture policy. It keeps the name of virtually all the brands it takes over – Coutts, NatWest, etc. So everywhere it goes it offers consumer choice. There is no overriding name.

Which is the better branding policy? Although you can argue it in every different direction it isn't an exam, there is no right answer. To make a decision, look at the marketplace, potential gaps in the market, assess in detail the brand portfolio, the company ambition, the core idea and weigh up the pros and cons of each possibility. Then make the choice.

Another modification of the brand architecture principle is the way some organizations, particularly airlines, attempt to create specific and clear sub-brands within the corporate whole. British Airways has First, Club World, World Traveller and other sub-brands, all quite clearly delineated operations within the single corporate BA brand.

Some companies following a branded policy don't seem to be disturbed by the fact that the corporate name is also the name of one of its brands. There are quite a few companies like this – Volkswagen, Ford and Pepsi. Other organizations go to great lengths to separate their corporate name from all their brand names, e.g. Altria owns brands such as Marlboro and Benson & Hedges.

Most organizations start with one name, one identity, one brand. However, as businesses grow they may make acquisitions, and these acquisitions may in turn own several companies or brands, and they then have to decide what to do with the names they have acquired. For example, DaimlerBenz acquired Chrysler, changed the corporate name and corporate brand to DaimlerChrysler, presumably to give the impression of a merger between equals, and allowed Chrysler to keep all its brands – Dodge, Jeep and so on, with consequences that I refer to later (see p. 57). On the other hand, Air France bought KLM but kept the brand. France Telecom acquired Orange, and also kept the brand. Nestlé acquired Rowntree, who in turn

possessed a number of product brands, like KitKat.
Nestlé kept the individual product brands but got
rid of the Rowntree corporate brand.

What these examples indicate is that the
breakdown between monolithic, endorsed and
branded architecture is helpful as a guide but no more.
They also indicate that there is no overall best way.
Each brand architecture model has advantages and
disadvantages. None is intrinsically superior to any
of the others. Each is appropriate in different
circumstances. When circumstances change, it may
sometimes be appropriate to change or modify brand
architectures. Finally, the examples indicate that there
is an infinite amount of modification and modulation
available within each system.

Take away

– Does your organization have clear
  brand architecture?
– If so, what is it?
– If it doesn't, is there a good reason
  for the present state of affairs?
– What can you do about it?

Section 3 – Why and When to Introduce Branding

Some brands are created from scratch. There was nothing there before – like Orange the mobile phone business, or Vueling the Spanish low-cost airline, or First Direct the internet bank, or perhaps the most famous example, Lexus the luxury car brand. More often, though, brands are reinvented. If it's there already, if it exists, if it has recognition and for one reason or another it has to be changed, then it's a reinvented brand. Or sometimes it just needs refreshing. There is, of course, a vast difference between invented and reinvented brands.

Invented brands

Where nothing exists except a business plan, there is no baggage: no name, no reputation, no staff, no prejudices for or against. But of course there are no customers and no market share; no sales either. So although starting from scratch is a huge opportunity, it's also a huge challenge. Get it wrong, and you lose a fortune and die. Get it right – like Orange, Vueling, First Direct or Lexus – and you smell of roses. Inventing brands from scratch, from nothing, is exciting, difficult, usually takes a long time to work and the opportunity doesn't happen often.

Lexus sprang forth from nothing – a classic invented brand.

Reinvented brands

Much more frequently existing brands are reinvented or refreshed, because the world in which they operate has changed or is changing. With an existing brand that needs reinventing, a culture already exists, together with a tradition, an attitude and a reputation, often a long-standing one. There are employees, customers, shareholders, suppliers. And there's also a name. So why tinker with what already exists?

The spirit of the times changes. Technologies change, fashions change; takeovers, mergers, globalization, all these affect business – and therefore businesses and their brands have to change too, sometimes just in order to occupy the same space in the minds of customers, the market and the world. Just standing still while the world changes around you is not an option. You end up an anachronism, like the Boy Scout movement did. And that's why organizations reinvent themselves. It's why they rebrand, both themselves as corporations and as the brands they own.

So how much should you change? Rebranding an entire corporation is much more complex than refreshing or reinventing one of its brands. That's why in this section I'm going to focus on the corporation as a whole.

If the entire organization is moving in a new direction – merging, acquiring, divesting, being privatized, going through massive technological and cultural change – the probability is that the corporate brand will need to shift and be seen to shift.

Technological and regulatory changes, often leading to consolidation, takeovers and mergers, affect industries on a massive scale. Look at the changes

BT keeps on reinventing itself. The piper is about talking; the globe embraces multimedia communications.

In Britain, Banco Santander appears under the acquired Abbey name but dresses in the corporate 'house style'.

Changes in business strategy and mergers and de-mergers entail corresponding changes in identity. These can go so far as to save a company from disaster – which happened when Andersen Consulting became Accenture.

DAIMLER BENZ

↓

DAIMLER CHRYSLER

↓

DAIMLER

in the financial service business and the emergence of a few massive global players. I've already mentioned HSBC and RBS, but they aren't alone. The Spanish bank, Banco Santander, has taken over Totta in Portugal and Abbey in the UK as well as a number of financial service businesses in Latin America. In each case, the new management needs to create a single back office, a single technological structure, a single purpose, a single set of behaviour patterns, and then has to consider whether to keep, change or discard the brands it has acquired, which leads ultimately to a single core idea and sometimes a single global brand, which may in turn lead to name changes.

Sometimes, however, relatively minor evolutionary shifts are in order. Shell has modulated its brand over the last hundred years or so just to keep more or less in the same place. In that case you can say the brand is being refreshed rather than reinvented. As a general rule the organization needs continuously to monitor its brands and, depending on the industry in which it operates, it may need to refresh them every decade or so.

Name changes

Name changes are perhaps the most contentious and high-profile of all branding issues. Nobody enjoys changing names; it's easy to attack the corporation for being self-indulgent and the new name, whatever it is, for being just silly. The time to consider changing a name, however, is either when the old name is badly tarnished, or when it is misleading, or when two companies come together and you need to draw a line and start again. Most companies, will go to very great lengths to avoid changing names. Name changes are expensive and complex and they are almost always ridiculed in the media when they are first announced. But sometimes when two great companies get together, like Guinness and GrandMet, a name change (in this case to Diageo) prevents, or at least inhibits, the emergence of badly bruised egos with an attendant fall in morale from damaging the newly formed organization.

Sometimes name changes can even save the company. When Andersen Consulting finally broke with its sister company, Andersen, at that time (1989) the world's largest accounting firm, both organizations went their separate ways. The agreement was that

Andersen Consulting would adopt a new and different name, hence Accenture launched in January 2001. In retrospect it's clear that this was probably the best single decision the old Andersen Consulting ever made. Changing its name almost certainly saved the organization from being brought down by the humiliation, disgrace and collapse of its former stable mate, which was destroyed in the fall-out of the Enron catastrophe.

So changing names isn't always so silly after all. In fact sometimes it's very sensible.

At times dodging the issue makes everything worse. When DaimlerBenz acquired Chrysler Corporation in 1998, both sides pretended it was a merger of equals – hence the new corporate name DaimlerChrysler. But the truth was that Chrysler was a sick company and under the thin veneer of an equal partnership DaimlerBenz tried to cure it. Chrysler's pretensions to equality made matters worse. The newly formed DaimlerChrysler Corporation was living a lie. It couldn't last. Eventually Daimler walked away and sold the business. Now its corporate name is Daimler AG.

The trigger for change

Changes in branding are not commissioned on the basis of a whim. There's always a reason. It might be increased competition leading to loss of market share, but what lies behind that? Looking and feeling out of date, changes in fashion, internal complacency leading to poor performance, a merger or takeover, or a new CEO who wants to make a fresh start....

It might simply be a recognition that the organization has until now taken its brand or brands for granted, not invested in them, not looked after them, and for this reason is letting them gradually fade away. Whatever it is, there's always a trigger for change.

Take away

– Does your corporate name provide a satisfactory umbrella under which all your activities can operate?
– Is there any confusion between the names of your corporation and one or more of its brands?

 1900

 1904

 1930

 1948

 1955

 1961

 1971

 1995

 1999

As aesthetics change with the times, sometimes corporate identities need to change, too – in order to stay in the same place.

Customers called Federal Express 'FedEx' so in 1994 the company officially changed its name to follow suit. Later, it added a ground service and a retail presence (with the acquisition of Kinko's, which had a strong enough brand name to warrant keeping it).

Section 4 – The Brand as a Corporate Resource

If it is effectively introduced and sustained, the brand is a major corporate resource – sometimes the organization's most significant financial asset. Like finance, investment, personnel, research and development, marketing, information technology and other corporate resources, the brand needs an appropriate power base, disciplines, adequate funding, commitment and management. If the brand resource receives this backing, it will operate just as effectively as any other corporate resource; if it doesn't, it will wither on the vine.

Leadership

The most significant prerequisite for making the brand work at its greatest potential is of course leadership. The chairman or CEO, or both, have overtly and demonstrably to support it. Because brands are intangible and because they are also often high-profile targets, some people who work inside the company get sceptical about their own brand. This leads directly to disaster.

If the boss stands up for the brand, and demonstrates with actions and not just words that he or she really believes in it, then it will get uncompromising support both internally and externally, even through difficult times. Great brands have immense capacity for survival – look at Marks & Spencer which went through a near-death experience – but they need to be led with conviction, financial support and an appropriate power base, which only top leadership can provide.

The importance and potential influence of a brand management system can be best understood by examining two other systems already functioning in the organization – financial management and information technology management.

Brand management

Brand management should be treated as a resource in every way equal to financial management or IT management – that is, as a corporate resource which will work effectively when it embraces every part of the organization.

Properly co-ordinated financial controls and the appropriate systems are rightly regarded as crucial, and the corporate financial system is seen as legitimate throughout every part of an organization. In some global institutions it is the financial management system, together with the IT system, that provides the glue which holds the entire corporation together. Financial management, with all its dedicated staff, its annual, monthly and even weekly rites of forecasting, budgeting, targeting and so on, is accepted unquestioningly as part of corporate life.

IT management is just as vital to the corporation. Over the past decades it has first invaded and then integrated itself into every corner of organizational life. An entire function has developed around assessing, satisfying and managing the organization's IT needs.

The Apple brand derives from, and is manifested in, everything the company does, from product design to packaging to architecture to in-store service.

The Brand as a Corporate Resource

Section 4

As it happens, really
powerful brands are
often 'authored' by
a visionary executive
like Steve Jobs.
Surprisingly often, too,
they derive strength
from their place of
origin. iPods say on
the back: 'Designed
by Apple in California'.

Part One

In fact IT has become so sophisticated and complex that it has come to dominate the actions, behaviour and structure of many of the organizations in which it is used. In banking and other financial service organizations, it is at least arguable that IT is the dominant function and largely determines the way in which the company does its business.

In today's world every department, from marketing to purchasing to human resources, should incorporate brand management into its thinking, behaviour patterns and actions. In some areas brand management will have a warmish welcome. In others, though, the welcome will initially be frosty because the new methodology will be seen to threaten an existing culture. Only if an organization takes its brand management truly seriously will it achieve its maximum potential. When a subsidiary company or brand has had a completely independent name and visual style, there is very often deep resentment when management proposes that a new corporate or branding style be adopted. Subordinate organizations sometimes go through the most complex avoidance procedures to wriggle out of change. 'You will ruin our business if you change the name/colour – or typeface.'

On a different level, purchasing departments may also present a dilemma. They operate on criteria that are usually intended to produce an appropriate level of quality at the lowest possible price. This may mean squeezing suppliers and therefore their employees very hard indeed, which may be inappropriate within the overall context of the corporate ethos. All this creates paradox and sometimes contradictory behaviour internally.

The internal contradictions are hard to handle, as BP and various other organizations claiming moral superiority have found. So there's plenty of opportunity for misunderstanding. But thorough brand management means consistent, coherent, congruent behaviour everywhere and with all corporate contacts, and this means working out and then putting into practice behaviour patterns that genuinely conform to the claims you make. In other words it means that with a well-integrated brand management system, the corporation has to put up or shut up.

Take away

- How seriously does your organization take brand management?
- Is every part of the business aligned to treat all of the organizations and people it deals with in a consistent way?
- Are there any parts of the business that resist the overall brand management value or visual system, because they claim to be different? If there are, are their claims valid?

PART TWO

Making Brands Work

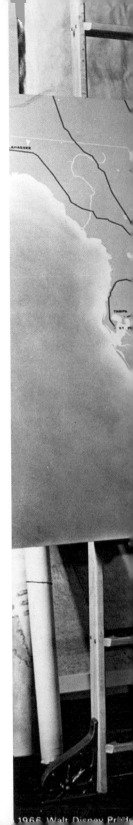

1966 Walt Disney Pr...

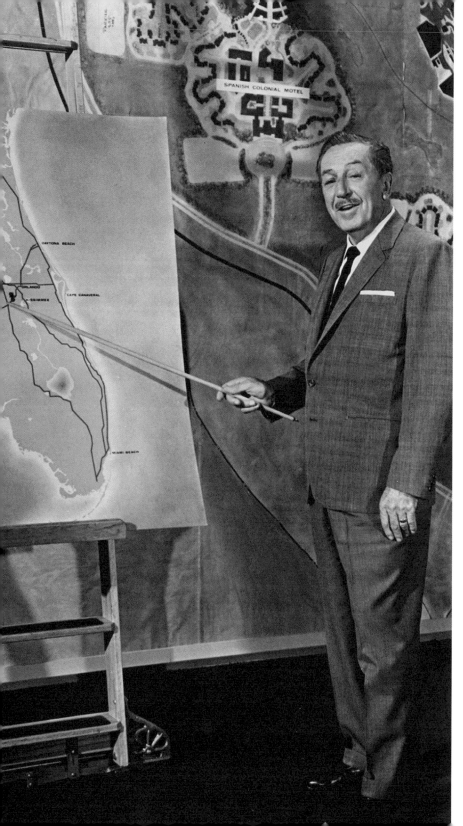

Walt Disney: a man
with an eye – and the
world's best-known
pair of mouse ears –
for branding.

Section 5 – Developing the Branding Programme

This section – based on years of experience – outlines how to create, launch, implement and manage a branding programme. Each stage is described in some detail, from the decision to go ahead, the level of commitment required and the appointment of consultants, to the methods of control, the various stages of work and the different ways of managing the brand, both formal and informal. If you follow the broad outline of what is proposed, you won't go far wrong. But evidently just as each organization is different, so each programme should vary. You may therefore need to modify and modulate some of the steps that follow to suit your particular purpose. In other words, what follows is a guide, and not an instruction manual.

Starting up and managing the programme

The next few sections which describe the process are based on the assumption that what is being changed is the corporate brand, because this is the most complex and far-reaching activity, although modifications and modulations of the process are appropriate for endorsed and branded architecture models.

The preliminaries

Large-scale branding programmes are relatively rarely commissioned. The organization committing itself to a branding programme for the first time may not be fully aware of its implications, and there is not necessarily a requirement to make a massive commitment all at once. It may be easier for some companies to enter into the process on a step-by-step basis. Sometimes one part of an organization may commission a branding project just to put a toe in the water.

Before the programme is commissioned it is very important for the chairman or chief executive to have a clear idea of what they want to achieve in the longer term. Is it part of a complete corporate turnaround? Is it to re-invigorate, re-inspire and create more cohesion internally? Is it to project a clearer series of ideas about the organization externally? Is it to make the company better known, to improve quality of recruits and make acquisitions easier? Is it to push up the share price, or achieve some similar tactical objective? Is it about consolidating a series of mergers or takeovers? Do they want to start with a specific job – something that has to be done – and possibly move on from there? Do they want some modification and modulation of what currently exists? Or are there other factors involved? Whatever the case, as I have indicated earlier, it is absolutely vital that the people at the top of the organization are seen to be involved and committed in the long term and that they sign off the brief to the consultants.

What follows can only be a rough guide because branding programmes vary so much in their scope and content, but the methodology remains the same.

> It is very important for the people at the top to have a clear idea of what they want to achieve in the long term

Branding consultancies
are rapidly growing
in influence within
the communications
business

The need for professional help

Organizations are rarely sufficiently objective, self-aware or experienced in the appropriate disciplines to carry out a major branding programme without external assistance, so they will usually look to outside consultants for professional help.

The traditional communications partner for the large company was its advertising agency. Gradually, however, as the area of communications has become more complex, specialist agencies of various kinds have emerged, including branding consultants. Branding, or as they were formerly called, design consultancies, are rapidly growing in influence within the communications business. In many countries, as branding becomes more sophisticated, companies are increasingly turning to these specialist branding consultancies for aid.

The branding consultancy field itself is both expanding and mutating, and it is beginning to embrace a wide range of disciplines. Though brand consulting is still a largely craft-based activity, the consultants themselves vary a good deal. Many have a characteristic visual style and concentrate on design rather than strategy. Others employ a mix of graphic designers and web designers, together with strategy consultants, sociologists and other consultants of various kinds. Some focus on just one area – design of retail interiors, retail developments like shopping malls, or packaging design, for example.

Most branding consultancies are small and independent. Even the bigger ones have between twenty and forty people and just one or two offices. More often an individual designer sets up a business, makes a partnership with some other professionals on a freelance basis, and off they go.

In the last few years, however, there has been a further development. There are now a few consultancies, all part of major global communication groups, which have ten or more offices and up to eight hundred staff. Most of these consultancies claim to be multi-disciplinary. Although these big consultancies are very experienced and therefore 'safe', their work is often bland and unimaginative; they hide behind process to which they give complex jargon-ridden names, in an attempt to make it all a bit of a mystery.

The truth is that, however much process is involved, the best work comes from inspired creative thinking.

There are plenty of consultants to choose from. Consultants should be appointed on the basis of their track record, their personality, their comprehension of the problem, their range of disciplines, their presentations, their proposed working methods and, of course, on whether the personal chemistry between them and the client works. What they charge is of course a factor, but it's only one of many. When you are choosing between big and small consultancies, you have to make your mind up whether you pick a company that has done it ten times and has the experience, or whether you want a fresh pair of eyes and an open mind.

The best work comes from inspired creative thinking

Take away
— What sort of branding consultants would suit my company? A one-man band, a medium-sized business, or one of the giants?
— Who am I actually going to deal with?
— Does the personal chemistry between us work?
— Do I understand what I am going to get for my money?

Creating two levels of control
Let us assume for the purposes of this guide that consultants have been appointed and that the programme will be a major operation involving a significant corporate turnaround. In this case it is run from the top and managed from the middle levels of the organization. As I have already pointed out, without overt commitment from the top, the programme may not get properly off the ground. It certainly won't become a viable management resource. But the programme also needs tight middle-management control; without this, it may founder and sink without trace. When a branding programme has been decided upon, the chairman

It is essential to clarify the brief and sort out the team as early as possible

or chief executive should appoint an executive to manage it who will directly report to him or her. Such a person will often have a design, communication, marketing or human resources background. It's helpful if he/she has had some experience of the branding process.

Because of the varying nature of branding work it is essential to clarify the brief and sort out the team as early as possible. For example, the creation, launching and implementation of a corporate branding programme demands different skills, disciplines and methodologies and therefore, to some degree, a different team from that for a programme directed at launching a new product or service brand.

Creating a steering group and working party
The key thing is that the programme has to be managed. So there has to be a visible and significant power base, which looks after costs, timing, output and deliverables. After the consultants have been appointed, the first job is to create the power base from which the project will be controlled. These mechanisms for control are the steering group and working party.

The steering group, headed by the chairman, CEO or some similar individual, consists of a small group of one or two divisional or resource heads together with the consultant leading the project. The job of the steering group is to monitor the overall progress of the job; to analyze, comment on and where appropriate approve, presentations at the various stages of work – and above all to see to it that it fits the brief.

The working party which reports to the steering group is headed by the executive nominated to be in charge of the project. The working party may be quite large, say up to eight people, not all of whom will necessarily be present at every meeting. This group will comprise executives of various levels from various parts of the organization and representatives of the consulting team – the project manager, strategic consultants, creatives with various special skills, and so on.

Informing the company

Before any interviews begin, the chairman or CEO should send a brief email to everyone in the organization saying that an evaluation of the corporate brand is taking place, consultants have been appointed and individuals from the company may be asked to take part in interviews and workshops on a confidential basis.

The stages of work

The work is divided into different stages, usually no more than seven. Individual consultancy approaches vary, but the process is always very similar. In this guide I have chosen four stages because I find it is simpler both to explain and understand:

STAGE ONE – investigation, analysis and strategic recommendations

STAGE TWO – developing the identity or brand idea (the look and feel)

STAGE THREE – launch and introduction (communicating the vision)

STAGE FOUR – implementation (making it happen).

These stages assume that the programme starts at the beginning, goes on to the middle and finishes at the end. But in some branding programmes, as work becomes more complex and sophisticated, this may not happen. Parts of the programme may be left out, new parts introduced, and so on. The pattern outlined in the pages that follow should therefore be treated only as a guide. You have to tailor the programme to suit the specific situation.

Tailor the stages of the programme to suit the specific situation

Stage One – investigation, analysis and strategic recommendations

The first activity is to get a full briefing and plan the project in detail. This ensures that everyone involved shares the same understanding and expectations, and that the right people are involved from the start.

From this a project plan is produced to include streams of work, detailed activities, timings for each phase and key milestones. This is then reviewed, amended, finalized and issued to the working party.

Next there is an intensive interview programme, a series of audits and appropriate desk research. These are the overall issues which should be addressed:

The first activity is to get a full briefing and plan the project in detail

— Nature of the industry/sector in which the organization operates: industry/sector size, growth patterns, profitability, rates of change, competition, changing technology, opportunities for growth, environmental concerns and corporate culture.
— The organization itself and its characteristics. First: size, position, profitability, market share, competitiveness, product quality, advertising, distribution, level of IT sophistication, and attitudes to corporate and environmental responsibility.
Second: perceptions about the organization's personality, core values, central idea and vision.
— Brands, businesses and divisions: how the different brands, products and services of the organization and its totality are seen and understood by different audiences. What each part of the business thinks about all the other parts and the centre.
— What its other outside stakeholders, customers, suppliers, partners, shareholders, commentators, unions, central and local government, and other audiences think and say about it.

Desk research
The desk research involves looking at the organization's history and structure: how it grew, who were the influential personalities and what were the significant events in its history. There may also be a lot of information about the position of competitors. In addition the organization may have carried out research about customers, social/cultural/industry trends, and so on.

Interviews and workshops
The interviews are intended, first, to gain insights and determine to what extent there is a consensus about the organization and, second, to uncover the issues that both unite and divide it.

The interviews embrace individuals representing different points of view, both inside and outside the organization. Interviews are normally, but not always, carried out by the brand consultants. The number of interviews will vary according to the size and complexity of the organization, from a minimum of 10–20 up to 100+.

Internal interviews

The interview programme is not intended to be statistically significant but it should be representative. Interviewees should be selected from all levels and all parts of the company. They should reasonably represent the age/sex profile of the organization. They should represent all shades of opinion about the proposed rebranding programme. They should certainly embrace some of those who are likely to be sceptical, as well as some of those who are neutral and then may be in favour of it.

Interviews should be confidential and loosely structured. Although interviewers must be clear about the issues they are examining, they need not follow a set questionnaire. The tone of the meetings should be cordial and informal.

The responses of internal interviewees will be conditioned by their role, responsibilities and length of service.

Each sector will have a view of its own significance and of the competence, loyalty and roles of the other divisions, brands and services of the corporation. All the divisions will have a view of the centre. These views are sometimes highly critical. People working in newer acquisitions will express different views from those in older businesses. Nationals of the 'home country' of the company may have different views from people in overseas operations. And so on. It's a rich field.

On the issue of name and visual style, people from some divisions or countries may say that controlling their own name and identity is vital to success in their markets. In my experience this is an issue on which individuals can become highly charged and emotional.

Respondents quite often find it hard to discuss abstract issues like vision or core idea. They are more likely to respond to questions on morale, leadership and clarity of purpose. They will be able to describe what it is like to work in the organization; whether it is hierarchical or egalitarian. In addition, they will be able to talk about its performance; its strengths and weaknesses in product/service quality, distribution, safety systems, competitiveness or other pertinent matters.

Interviews and workshops aim to gain insights, determine consensus and uncover issues

Other issues may emerge. For example, intellectual property and patents are becoming increasingly important.

People at the centre normally have their own perspective about the loyalties, ability and significance of each division.

Workshops

In some organizations, especially those which are operating across a number of product fields in many countries, it's useful to conduct workshops. Each workshop might have up to one hundred participants drawn from different divisions of the organization and at different levels of seniority. The goals behind the workshops are:
— To explain what branding really is and how individuals taking part in the workshop can help to shape the brand.
— To raise the profile of the whole programme internally and get people on side.
— To elicit internal views and input that, in addition to helping influence the nature of the brand, may deal with a number of issues, e.g. brand copyright and other legal or technical matters, which could affect the proposed outcome.

External interviews

External interviews should be conducted with suppliers, customers, competitors, collaborators, journalists and, where appropriate, representatives from other groups like government and trade associations. Interviewees must be selected to ensure a representative sample.

The purpose of these interviews is to find out how much outsiders know about both the mechanics of the company (size and profitability, ownership and products, services and other skills), what their views are about its strengths, weaknesses and impact on the outside world, and what image, attitudes and overall perceptions they may have about the organization. In other words, the purpose of the external interviews is to examine the corporate reputation.

Interviewees should be given only the most general idea of the purpose of the interview, if anything at all. Sometimes it helps not to reveal the purpose of the interview. It may pay to be oblique.

External interviews are useful in different ways from internal interviews. Often they reveal as much about what outsiders don't know as what they do. Sometimes outsiders know an organization and its industry very well. Generally, though, people outside a company have a partial and distorted view of it. They often know very little about its products or geographical spread. This does not of course inhibit them from expressing quite emphatic views. Incidents which took place some years ago may still influence them. For example, a corporate financial scandal or a product-quality problem like Coca-Cola's difficulties in Belgium may hang around in the air for years after it has been resolved, and the people involved have long gone.

Even in the financial world, where analysts are paid to dissect a company's structure and performance, there is often a great deal of misunderstanding and misinformation, so interviewers should expect some distortion. But even a slanted picture reveals a great deal about perceptions and reality. Remember in these interviews we are specifically looking for perceptions.

It is the combination of internal and external interviews that so often gives such an interesting picture.

Audits

Then there are the five audits – for communications, behaviour, design, brand architecture and competitors. Emphasis will be placed on each according to their significance within the whole programme.

The communications audit

The communications audit examines what the organization says, to whom and how, and whether it uses a consistent tone of voice. It also examines whether the organization listens: to its own people, and to outsiders; to dealers, suppliers, investors and customers.

Areas to examine are:
— How the communication system works and who manages what.

Audits examine what the organization says, how it says it, to whom it says it – and how hard it listens back

Fundamental attitudes towards people both inside and outside the organization must be examined

— The links (if any) between internal and external communications.
— Content, quality and consistency of external and internal communications.
— Whether all appropriate audiences are adequately covered.
— How the organization communicates with its employees and, where appropriate, with other quasi-internal organizations (although this is partly a behavioural issue).
— Whether there is a consistent tone in which the organization communicates. And if so, what is it? Friendly? Formal? Jargon-ridden?
— How it deals with outside partners and suppliers, some of whom are so close to it that for practical purposes they may seem to form part of the company.

At the same time as it looks at its internal communications, the audit team should consider how the organization deals with its external audiences through press and public relations, annual reports, display and TV advertising, and other formal and informal channels. How does it handle digital? The internet, the intranet, blogs and all other digital channels of communication come under scrutiny. Does the organization understand the power of the web? What is its own web content like? Do people blog about it? Does it respond to blogs?

As part of the audit process, the technical and general media should be reviewed in order to see how the group and its activities are perceived.

An audit of this kind is particularly important in an organization comprising a large number of smallish units, like a bank with its widespread branch network, or an automobile manufacturer with a network of independently owned dealers. In this situation what people in the various units are told, about what is going on and when, directly affects what they feel about the organization.

The behavioural audit
Much of the feedback regarding the way in which people within a company interact both internally and with the various external groups with whom they deal, can be derived from the interview programme, the workshops and the other audits,

but in some cases a specific audit on corporate attitudes will be required.

Here are some issues to consider:

— Does the company invest in the development of people?
— Does it set personal performance objectives and does it appraise performance regularly?
— Does it reward people in relation to their performance?
— Is there a genuine commitment to service, value and long-term relationships, or merely lip service?
— Is it trustworthy in honouring its commitments?
— Is it a good neighbour?
— How does it react to criticism both from internal and external sources?
— Does it manifest any principles not directly relevant to business?
— Does it act in the way that it talks?
— Does it treat people in the 'home' country differently from the rest?

Questions on this topic are intended to reveal fundamental attitudes.

Sometimes the audit team may have access to customer opinion/satisfaction research, in which case a parallel enquiry can deal with the way the organization is seen to behave:

— What are the different parts of the organization like to deal with?
— How helpful are the staff in answering questions and resolving problems?
— How quickly are customers served or telephone calls answered?
— Are its representatives polite or rude, or does their performance vary?

In a service activity like a police force, an airline or a logistics company, this audit must be given considerable weight. In addition, in this type of audit, interviews with customers – especially dissatisfied customers – can be very revealing.

The design, or visual, audit

The primary purpose of this audit is to examine the way in which different parts of the organization present themselves in terms of their physical presence. An example of everything that the organization produces must be collected and examined for consistency, coherence and cost. At the same time, the team should visit a representative example of different buildings, sites, showrooms, stores and offices which the organization occupies.

When senior management examines examples of the totality of the corporate output with all its inevitable inconsistencies and contradictions, it usually has a salutary and disturbing impact and reinforces the need for coherence.

The brand architecture audit
When an organization has a particularly complex brand architecture, with subsidiaries with different names in different countries, where there is a great deal of co-branding or a similar set of issues, a specific brand architecture audit may be appropriate.

This audit covers all existing brands, sub-brands, names and descriptions, as well as their perception, function and place in the brand hierarchy. It may also cover co-branding, joint ventures and other variants.

The audit helps to show how brands are organized, what the hierarchies are, how close the relationships between brands and the whole corporation are, where there is a requirement for clearer lines of demarcation, and so on.

An examination of main brands, subsidiaries, co-brands, joint ventures – and all competitors in key markets – may be appropriate

The competitor audit
It is important to carry out an audit of major competitors in key markets. The audit should cover their websites, media comments, marketing literature, advertising and all other appropriate areas.

Findings
When all the audits, the interviews and most of the workshops have been carried out, the working party, which will have been meeting regularly, debates the findings.

Working party meetings should have taken place regularly on a formal basis, say once a month, and informally more frequently. During these meetings the detailed recommendations will have been thrashed out. After discussion, the findings and recommendations are formally presented to the smaller steering group and then the board. The outside consultancy almost always prepares and makes the presentation in consultation with the working party and steering group. This process can take between two and four months depending on the size of the organization and the scope of the interview/audit programme.

The presentation

It is important to take into account that branding is likely to be an unfamiliar, even alien, subject to many of the board members to whom the consultants will present, and they should therefore take care to make their presentation clear, logical, relevant and comprehensive. Even though the presentation may have been thoroughly considered both by the working party and the steering group, it is unwise, at least in my experience, to regard the board presentation as a formality.

A presentation of findings should start by recalling the brief: 'This is what we were asked to do.' It should go on to describe what the team did. Then what they found. And then: 'This is the action that we recommend.' In this way the consultancy can explain in a step-by-step fashion how it has arrived at its conclusions. It can justify and explain what it thinks should be done next.

The salient issues must be explained clearly, succinctly and with ample evidence. Suppose a large worldwide organization is under scrutiny; suppose also that it has grown by acquisition and has a plethora of companies, each with its own ethos, product and service brands engaged in different activities. And suppose further that the organization is perceived internally to be uncoordinated, lacking a clear sense of direction, with overlapping and unclear lines of responsibility, with no clear personnel policy and products of varying quality. Suppose, in other words, that it is perceived internally as a bit of a shapeless mess.

The likelihood is that external audiences will reflect a similar picture. Outsiders will only know bits of the organization, its size and scale will be underrated and its reputation will vary dramatically according to the part that people know – and so on.

If this is how the organization is perceived, then this perception, however unpalatable, has to be clearly laid out and backed by appropriate evidence

Presentations should be clear, logical, relevant and comprehensive both from the desk research interviews, workshops and audits.

Recommendations

Findings – in other words, how the organization is perceived, and why it is perceived that way – must be accompanied by recommendations for action.

The core idea

During the course of the investigation, the sector in which the organization operates will have been considered as a whole. The special characteristics of the organization – those characteristics that make it unique and different from its competitors – should also have emerged. Equally the opportunities for the organization, its ambitions, or the ambitions of many of its leading personalities, will have been explored. In addition, marketing opportunities and the positioning that the organization and its various component parts could adopt will have to be taken into account.

This is the opportunity for the organization to play to its strengths: to develop a core idea which reveals its personality, and a vision which emphasizes its sense of purpose and which helps it to seize the marketing high ground.

This core idea must be put forward at the presentation, discussed in detail, where necessary modified, further discussed and ultimately agreed and encapsulated in writing. Sometimes, in fact quite often, it takes two or three meetings to get agreement.

When it's all agreed, one side of typing paper should normally be quite enough to outline what the company's core idea is, what it does, how it does it and what its vision for its future is. This brief document must avoid clichés, get to the heart of the matter, and outline a concept which is both unique to the organization and recognized as grounded in its realities by those who work for and deal with it.

This core idea must form the basis on which the whole branding programme is developed. It is vital to the whole operation to get it right and then get it agreed and signed off.

Following the development of and agreement to the core idea, the second stage of work can begin.

> An organization should play to its strengths, reveal its personality and emphasize its sense of purpose

Example

When the Spanish oil company Repsol was formed in the 1980s from the autarchic state monopoly Instituto Nacional de Hidrocarburos (INH), which constituted virtually the entire Spanish energy sector, the core idea emerged naturally from the new positioning. Spain had just entered the European Union, and the world's major oil companies had the opportunity of entering the hitherto protected Spanish domestic market in which INH was the only significant player. The company had to defend its position in Spain. INH had to be revitalized and eventually privatized.

Because of its size, as one of Spain's largest companies, its high-profile presence in every town and on every main highway in the country, and because of its competitive position as Spain's chief player in the global oil world, Repsol had the opportunity to become the admired model for a revitalized, dynamic, commercially aggressive and democratic Spain. Repsol could become and be seen as the new Spain's industrial and commercial flagship. This was the core idea that was presented to and agreed by the board. This vision was made overt and explicit and became the brief upon which the new corporate brand was based.

The naming structure and visual interpretation of the brand followed from this brief. The name INH was abandoned in favour of one of the brands, Repsol, which became the corporate brand. This gave the organization strength and coherence. So traditional names in chemicals, exploration and distribution were abandoned; a move which caused considerable but temporary pain. The new visual idea had to be Spanish in feeling and appearance, but it also had to present the strength and sophistication of a major global oil company. It was launched as part of a massive and on-going internal and external communication programme, in which a series of powerful, clear and simple messages were reiterated. The corporate branding programme ran in parallel with a long-term behavioural change programme.

Twenty years later, although Repsol has grown, absorbed Argentina's YPF and developed into a worldwide energy player, it remains one of a handful of hugely admired Spanish global businesses, and with some minor modulations along the way has retained the visual identity created two decades ago, because the core idea was and remains relevant to corporate ambitions.

Stage Two – development of the identity
As a result of the work carried out in the first stage, culminating in the presentation and the agreement of the core idea, actions may be taken on the three interrelated areas:
— Behavioural change
— Brand architecture
— Name and visual style.

Behavioural change
There may be a requirement to develop a behavioural change programme based around the need to promulgate the new core idea internally.

The process of introducing and managing behavioural change can be complex, difficult and prolonged. Depending on the size of the organization and the level of change required, such a process can take up to three years.

A wide variety of organizational behaviour disciplines is available to corporations. Specialist consultants should be appointed to work on these issues.

Brand architecture
Issues to examine here are:
— Do we have or should we develop a corporate, endorsed or branded system of architecture?
— How do we make it work?
Sometimes, as in the case of Repsol, it's pretty clear what to do, even though it might need drastic surgery to do it. More often, though, the issues are complex and multi-faceted. Each possible solution has to be explored, and its advantages and drawbacks weighed up. For more detail refer to Section 2 (see p. 44).

Name and visual style
Linked to brand architecture is name and visual style. Should there be some change in what the organization is called, how it looks and presents itself; either a minor change involving modification to the existing identity or something entirely new?

A new core idea can be promoted with behavioural change, brand architecture change or a change in name and visual style

Name

Name changes mark dramatic shifts in the fortunes or situation of organizations. Nations provide instructive examples. Many former colonies have changed their name after going independent. The Dutch East Indies became Indonesia in the late 1940s after three hundred years of Dutch colonial rule and a bitter and bloody struggle. More recently new nations have emerged or previously submerged nations have re-emerged: Ukraine, Slovenia, Slovakia, Montenegro, Kazakhstan, Serbia and Croatia are all new or reborn nations with unfamiliar names in the wider world.

In the commercial world the issues are similar. New names emerge either at times of profound change both in reality and self-image or when a new brand is launched; sometimes the change is abrupt and radical.

Example

El Banco Deuno was the name created for a new Mexican bank. Accelerated growth, low inflation, a stable job market, expanding credit and liberal trade had led to the sense of a new prosperity in Mexico, which in turn led to the emergence of a confident, demanding and educated middle class. El Banco Deuno was to be their bank: a new bank for the new Mexico, and a byword for progress, inclusion and optimism. The name of the bank had to play an important role in expressing the corporation's democratic nature. It came from the combination of two Spanish words, 'de' and 'uno', meaning 'of' and 'one', i.e. 'one's'. Combined with the word 'Banco', the name reads as 'one's bank' – in other words, 'my bank and everybody's bank'.

Like symbols, names are emotive. Creating and introducing a new name is difficult and complex for the following reasons:
— First, names have no real life or meaning until they are put into context, so it is extremely difficult for the people going through the naming or renaming process to appreciate the power of the name they have chosen until well after the event, when it has taken on a life of its own.
— Second, this is a subjective issue. Individual preferences and feelings are very important.

Creating and introducing a new name can be an emotive and challenging issue

— Third, a very large number of names are already registered and it is increasingly difficult to find 'free names'.
— Fourth, names are a legal minefield. Name registration is complex and rights to the ownership of names are sometimes difficult to determine. Many names are owned, part-owned or can be claimed by organizations whose legal position is debatable. The legal processes involved in name change can be vexatious and contentious.

Having said all that, there are, as always, a few naming guidelines which might be helpful.

Types of name

Names can be classified under the following types:
— First is the name of an individual or individuals, usually the company's founder like Ford, Philips, Honda, Marks & Spencer, Siemens and Tata.
— Second come descriptive names like British Airways or General Motors. Currently anything with the prefix Euro is fashionable. Remember though, that descriptive names can become embarrassingly outdated: there was once a grocery chain called Home & Colonial Stores.
— Third are abbreviated names like Conoco and FedEx.
— Fourth are initials, for example KLM, IBM and BP.
— In the fifth category are names like Kodak, which have no meaning but are simply intended to look and sound unique and attractive.
— In the sixth category are conceptual names – that is, names that try to give an impression of what the organization seeks to do or to be, e.g. Jaguar, Accor, Volvo – or Yoigo.

Example

Yoigo is a Spanish mobile phone company, launched with the help of Saffron in 2006. The word 'Yoigo' is an idiomatic and emphatic way of saying 'I hear' in Spanish.

— Finally there are those names that capture a mood. These may be nonsensical (Yahoo or Google), or their original meaning may be subverted (Virgin), but they are powerfully evocative.

Criteria for selecting a name

The name should:
— Be easy to read
— Be easy to pronounce, preferably in any language
— Have no disagreeable associations, preferably
   in any language
— Be suitable for use as the organization expands
   into different activities
— Be registrable, or at least protectable
— Not date – or become old-fashioned
— Be idiosyncratic
— Be something with which a powerful visual style
   can be associated
— Have charisma
— In addition, it may sometimes be desirable for it
   to relate to the activity of the company.

It's pretty well impossible for any name to fill all
these criteria, but we all keep trying.

One last thought on names. Branding
programmes involving name changes are difficult
and people get very worked up about it all. My
advice on changing names is simple. Don't – unless
you really have to.

Visual style

Some thoughts on symbols are outlined in Section 1
(see p. 30). Logos or symbols – as much as, perhaps
even more than, names – arouse deep and sometimes
conflicting emotions.

Organizations that have spent millions on
promoting their logos over years are more likely
to wish to modify what they have than change
completely – and they may well be right. Within
the last two decades Renault, one of Europe's
automotive giants, has modified its symbol and
all its other visual manifestations twice, but the
basic lozenge shape has remained. These
modifications are simply intended to help keep
the organization in the same place.

There are situations, however, when it may be
desirable to produce a new visual solution. This
is especially necessary when an organization is
introducing a new corporate vision or – to put it
another way – introducing a new core idea. But
timing is a critical issue: the new visual identity
must represent a new reality.

Logos and symbols,
as well as names,
can arouse deep and
conflicting emotions

Example

Round about the turn of the twenty-first century BP threw out its old logo – a quasi-military shield – and replaced it with a helix, when under CEO John Browne it began to reposition itself as an eco-friendly, green kind of energy company, of which perhaps the most dramatic or perhaps melodramatic interpretation was the advertising campaign 'Beyond Petroleum'.

Unfortunately, as it turned out, there was more style than substance in the BP rebranding programme. A series of disasters in some of the plants, including loss of life, turned it into a mockery. Which is a salutary reminder that a change of visual identity makes a promise of changed performance, which has to be fulfilled. The visual style must never promise more than the organization will be able to deliver. If it isn't delivered, the organization is deemed to be intending to mislead, as BP found out to its cost. The public and its spokespersons in the media are rightly unforgiving on this issue.

Design approaches

Once there is agreement on the extent of change required, the consultancy will prepare a series of optional design approaches which it will show on screen across an appropriate range of activities. Quite often up to three or more visual approaches are appropriate. These must be debated, first by the working party, then by the steering group, before they are finally presented to and agreed by the board.

The chosen design scheme is then worked up for a presentation showing how the various applications will work for the different disciplines within the business, as well as for all its different audiences: for example, applied to a business card, a brochure cover, a press advertisement or website homepage; also as signage on exteriors and interiors of buildings, on vehicles and uniforms; and of course where necessary how the applications work in co-branding situations.

The approved designs must be developed and then fine-tuned so that they are usable across a wide range of materials (e.g. plastics, paper, metal) and a wide range of sizes (e.g. buttonhole badges to neon signs) in a wide range of countries with differing technical facilities, by people inside and outside the company with varying skills, knowledge and interest.

After that a set of basic elements are produced from artwork (see Appendix A, p. 107).

From these basic elements a wide range of typical applications for use is prepared, covering, say, stationery, signs and shop interiors, and multimedia (see Appendix B, pp. 107–108).

Stage Three – launch and introduction

Communicating the vision is the key to creating and sustaining understanding of the new core idea that is to be driven through the corporate brand.

The launch of a new corporate brand gives management an opportunity to explain what the organization is, where it has come from, where it is going and how the new visual identity will help it get there. In other words, visual aspects of the brand become the vehicle that launches the programme.

For many organizations the launch of the new corporate brand can represent a rite of passage, a kind of rebirth, and it may therefore be appropriate to make it into an elaborate and ritualized occasion. On the other hand some organizations may feel that this theatrical approach is inappropriate to their ethos. Each organization must choose what is natural to it.

Internal launch

The internal launch of a branding programme takes place before the external launch, because people inside the organization have to know about it first if they are to feel that it is really theirs. If it is linked to a major organizational change, say a merger, involving a new name and brand, the various groups involved in the rebranding activity should have worked together to agree how to inculcate and explain the new core idea, spirit or vision. The internal launch of the new brand should be the climax of this process, and specialist events management companies who are highly skilled at creating this kind of activity should be appointed to do the work.

The internal launch normally takes the form of seminars, discussions and audiovisual presentations.

For many organizations the launch of the new brand can represent a rite of passage

Many of the world's great organizations devote much time and energy to communication

The level of razzamatazz varies from a complex and sophisticated presentation with all the high-tech skills of a world-class stage or TV show, complete with well-known personalities, to a much lower-key, more folksy, down-home activity. The level of launch chosen depends on the message, the corporate ethos and tradition, and similar matters.

Many of the world's great organizations now devote much time and energy to communication. Some companies have their own internal TV networks for dissemination of corporate policy, news of new launches and so on. Where significant communication channels exist, such as intranet and so on, they should be used as vehicles to launch the identity and propagate the core idea; where they don't exist, these communication channels should be created.

Partner/supplier launch

In an increasing number of businesses – automotive, aerospace, and so on – risk-sharing partners are so important that, even though they are outsiders, they are virtually insiders as well. At a more mundane level, if an outside security firm mans reception, then their people are in effect the public face of the institution and have to be treated as such.

The whole issue of the extent to which outsider suppliers should be treated as insiders and therefore take part in the launch process is tricky and has to be decided on an individual basis. What's clear is that it can't be ignored.

Dealer/distributor launch

Although dealers/distributors are not part of the corporate entity, their success – as in cars or soft-drink bottling – is often bound up with the fortunes of the organizations with which they deal. Launches to dealers are therefore much more akin to internal launches than those for external audiences.

External launch

Nobody should expect the outside world to be as interested in the new branding programme as insiders – even when it is deliberately aimed at creating a new corporate brand for customers. So be prepared for this. Quite often, though, if the organization is high-profile and the change radical, the media will pick up on it. How much did it cost? What is it for? And so on.

The external launch involves both traditional advertising and digital media, and often a quite complex media relations programme. It is sometimes suitable to use sophisticated audiovisual techniques at such events.

The appropriate consultants in advertising, public relations, multimedia events and so on must be co-opted into the programme to handle these activities.

Stage Four – implementation

Once the brand has been created and designed, all the tools necessary to ensure that the brand is clearly understood and consistently implemented are created. Guidelines will help manage the brand now and in the future. When it comes to documenting the brand idea and its execution, there are many different types of tool available, as well as different levels of detail in which each tool can be developed. Some follow below.

Brand guidelines

The guidelines will be used by a cross-section of internal people and outside contractors, from designers to signage makers to manufacturers, and so on. The guidelines need to be simple and robust to use, so a format has to be created to suit each individual client's requirements, and master artwork for logos has to be supplied (in formats for both Mac and PC).

Guidelines can include the following:
— logo – sizing and spacing
— colour – primary and secondary colour palettes
— typefaces
— tone of voice
— imagery
— stationery
— literature system principles
— PowerPoint style principles
— internal communication tools
— website and online applications – principles and templates
— office environments
— signage
— proposals and other key documents

Simple, robust guidelines will help manage a brand now and in the future

Brand centre (or intranet)

A brand centre is an online tool which captures everything about the brand, from the core idea to detailed instructions for its implementation.

It is a secure web page designed to assist brand users (both internal and external) and is also a very useful tool for creating a community of brand owners within an international organization.

Brand centres are very scaleable in terms of functions, structure, content, access privileges, and so on.

Brand guardianship

When the branding programme is first introduced, it has to be guarded and protected. This can either be done externally, through a retainer to the brand consultancy or internally through a brand manager, or indeed both.

Brand book

The objective is to create an inspiring, imaginative, yet clear and practical way of telling the brand story. It's a motivational tool for employees. It can be large or small in format, humorous or serious in tone (I've seen one like a Japanese Manga graphic book), but it must always characterize the organization, so that whoever picks it up or views it online knows what the brand is all about and feels inspired and excited.

Making change stick

When it is carried out thoroughly, the branding process is deeply satisfying because it does make change evident. If the programme is introduced and implemented wholeheartedly and enthusiastically, it will completely refocus and refresh the way in which the organization sees itself and is seen by others. It will also help the organization in its ambitions.

Managing implementation

As with any other corporate resource, the successful management of the corporate brand depends on the effort and enthusiasm with which it is introduced, managed and sustained. Because the corporate brand is a resource embracing products and services, environments, communication and

The objective of a brand book is to create an inspiring, imaginative, yet clear and practical way of telling a brand story

behaviour, each of which must be incorporated into the management process (see Section 1, p. 31), it has to be managed on the lines similar to those two other corporate resources, finance and information technology systems (see Section 4, p. 61). It has to be ubiquitous; it must penetrate every part of the organization; and it must be effective both in letter and spirit. In order to work, it has to have both formal and informal support systems.

Formal brand management systems

The formal implementation management programme will normally be based around a Head of Brand, who may also be Head of Design, Head of Communication or occasionally even Creative Director. Whatever he/she is called, this person will liaise with virtually all of the operating units and central functions.

The team has to oversee standards in signs, packaging, online and all other visual areas, including architecture. The team may have to work with partners on co-branding projects, or with sub-brands belonging to the organization. The team will work with suppliers of all kinds to create and sustain appropriate standards. The brand guidelines, whether electronic or in printed form, will be a fundamental tool of this team.

In addition, the brand will have an impact on all new activities of every kind, from commissioning a new building or refurbishing an existing one to acquiring a new subsidiary. As the organization changes, moves into new activities and develops new products, the brand must be used appropriately and modified where necessary.

From time to time there will be a conflict of interest or opinion. Many divisions or sectors will claim that they are different; they have particular reasons for things staying the way they are, for not accepting the new standards. There will be plenty of battles. As in any dispute between a corporate resource and a division, this should be resolved by arbitration.

Informal brand management

So much for the formal part of the programme. At a fundamental and in some ways more significant level, however, the branding programme is to do

The brand will have an impact on all activities of every kind, and must be used appropriately

Companies with a powerful and well-implemented brand know that the brand resource helps them achieve their objectives

with emotion; creating and sustaining a feeling about what is appropriate for the organization, demonstrating a consistency of purpose (see Section 1, p. 25). In the most successful branding programmes everything that the organization does or says represents what it is and underlines its identity. And this is not just because there is a formal policing structure, but because there is an all-pervasive spirit which everyone, or at least most people, within the organization intuitively understand. Any close examination of organizations that use their corporate brand effectively will confirm this. Companies with a powerful and well-implemented brand know that the brand resource helps them achieve their objectives, therefore they respect it; some may even treasure it. All this of course stems from the top. When the chairman or CEO guards the corporate brand and the core idea it stands for, and cherishes it, the rest of the organization follows. Nike is often and quite properly cited as an organization that guards all aspects of its brand with this kind of care.

In addition to this, the corporate brand which should so clearly outline the shape and structure of the organization and give visual expression to its strategy constantly reminds management where its goals lie, and what is and is not appropriate. As you may have noticed if you've been reading carefully, an effective branding programme is, I say it yet again, the corporate strategy made visible.

Flexibility

Does all this mean that the organization has to become an unwieldy, inflexible, invasive giant? Not if things are handled properly. There must always be room for individual initiative and enterprise and, in some cases, interpretation.

A good deal of criticism has been levelled at branding programmes for introducing a kind of bland homogeneity across everything that they touch. High streets are said to be increasingly similar; so are the world's airports. Much of this criticism is justified. In the world of oil companies, for example, simply to make every service station everywhere in the world look the same in the interest of immediate recognition and economies

of scale is to ignore, even to obliterate, the joy
that we all take in variety and difference and the
goodwill that consumers develop towards the
organization that offers them diversity. By the same
token it is neither necessary nor desirable for every
bank branch regardless of whether it is in a small
country town, a shopping mall or a major financial
centre to look exactly the same. There is a
compelling case for variety within consistency.

Some organizations are beginning to recognize
that diversity of offerings within a coherent
framework makes an attractive commercial offer.

Example
Leon, a new fast-food chain based around the simple
core idea of real food fast, makes each of its outlets
look subtly different and appropriate to the
surrounding environment within a coherent,
corporate context.

What's more, the interpretation of the core idea may
vary between one national culture and another.
Local interpretation is vital. A Chekhov play
performed in English is not, or should not be,
a literal translation of the Russian, but should
interpret its spirit. The same applies in branding.
It is the spirit that has to be interpreted.

Inevitably the brand will need to be modulated
and adapted from time to time according to
changing circumstances. Information technology
is making this opportunity for greater variety
and modulation readily available. In other words,
like every other management tool, branding has
to be used with discretion, care and an appropriate
flexibility.

Section 6 – Control, Cost and Timing

Costs and timings for branding programmes will vary, because every situation is different. The thing to remember is that the major cost in any branding programme is implementation. Consultancy costs are almost always relatively low in relation to implementation, particularly bearing in mind the potential significance of a branding programme. Where would Orange, for example, be without its brand? Compared to the cost of strategic and other consultants, too, branding consultancy comes fairly cheap, although as brands become more and more significant in the corporate mix, branding and consultancy costs will inevitably rise accordingly.

Methods of control and costing

When a brand is simply refreshed, there is normally no need to change all of the applications at once. Though buildings have to be painted, signs put up, vehicles acquired and put into appropriate livery, training undertaken, and so on, there is an existing schedule and budget for all of this, so for the most part the work can be embraced within and coordinated by the branding programme. There may not therefore be much new or additional expenditure (although there will of course be a major requirement for management time as part of a re-education and indoctrination process).

On the other hand, when there is a radical change – a new name, and entirely new look and feel – there may well be considerable extra costs, because everything has to be changed fast.

There are of course inevitably some costs – consultants' fees and launch costs, and there may be a massive advertising programme to promote the new, refreshed or reinvented brand. (Advertising is often still the most expensive aspect of a branding programme, although its distribution between digital and conventional media may have to be carefully evaluated.)

Corporate branding costs can often be dealt with as part of annual financial budgets

Budgeting

This means that when the modifications are not too radical, corporate branding costs can, apart from the origination work, often be dealt with as part of annual financial budgets. But as I have indicated, when a new or dramatically revised brand programme is initiated, an additional budget will almost certainly be mandated.

In addition to the changes in look and feel, there may well be extra costs in introducing and implementing behavioural change. Costs can be divided up and examined in the following way:
— Consultants' fees
— Cost of creating new materials (e.g. signs on buildings, websites)
— Cost of launching the brand (e.g. advertising, videos, DVDs and other media costs)
— Replacement costs – those costs involved in replacing existing materials which in fact would have needed replacing anyway (e.g. brochures, vehicle liveries, etc.)

— Costs for internal communication and training
Each programme should be costed in stages. A fixed
budget for time and fees should be established for
Stage One ('Investigation, Analysis and Strategic
Recommendations') and Stage Two ('Development
of the Identity'). Variations should be allowed for
if the brief changes. There should be a clear
separation between fees and outside costs. Fees for
Stage Three ('Launch and Introduction') and Stage
Four ('Implementation') should be negotiated as the
project develops and its total approximate size can
be estimated. During the course of Stage Three,
and more particularly during Stage Four, fees
should be negotiated for separate projects.

Controls

The corporate branding resource has to be
established with a clear brief, adequate funding
and appropriate lines of authority. Here are some
of the issues that have to be resolved:
— Who is going to pay for the programme – the
centre or the operating units?
— How should liaison between different companies
or sectors, geographic divisions and the central
brand resource work?
— How should the resource be manned and how
many staff should it have?
— Where should it be located?
— What should the lines of responsibility be?
A cost, time and method schedule for the launch and
subsequent management of the programme must be
prepared at the same time as detailed preparation
work is taking place. This will be monitored regularly,
and almost certainly modified from time to time.

Size, scope, speed and cost

At what speed is the implementation programme
going to be introduced and sustained? There are four
choices:
— An overnight change from old to new
— A controlled change taking place very quickly,
say over a period of a year
— A controlled but more gradual change, say over
three to five years
— Gradual replacement on an ad-hoc basis.

The corporate branding
resource has to be
established with a clear
brief, adequate funding
and appropriate lines
of authority

Quite reasonably most organizations like to keep costs down so where possible they will choose the longer, slower, cheaper option. However, the method chosen must depend on the nature of the brand change, as I indicated earlier (see p. 69). The more dramatic the change, the more rapidly the new brand should be introduced, and inevitably the higher the cost will be. If the existing identity is only modified, the introduction can be lower key, the programme of implementation more gradual, and therefore the costs can be lower and spread out over a longer period.

Example

Lloyd's of London is the best known and least understood insurance brand in the world. It's a 300-year-old insurance market where companies both collaborate and compete. The Lloyd's brand needed to be refreshed, and the challenge was to help keep the institution relevant and central in a rapidly growing and changing insurance market.

LLOYD'S

What made Lloyd's great was its unusual structure, which enabled it to devise solutions for risks that others shied away from. This approach, coupled with the trust and reassurance derived from several centuries of trading, was the paradox at the heart of the organization.

Lloyd's was also full of great stories and the refreshed brand created an opportunity to tell them in a distinctive way. The core idea that emerged was termed 'constant originality'. The Lloyd's logo was strengthened so that it could work alongside all the different insurance brands that trade in the Lloyd's market without dominating them.

The company started in a coffee shop. The Richard Rogers landmark Lloyd's building in London still has a coffee shop, but it's a bit different. Though Lloyd's operates in many places worldwide, its spirit of 'constant originality' is ubiquitous. Because the brand was refreshed rather than completely reinvented, the additional budget required was relatively modest. For the most part the refreshed brand emerged within existing budgets.

PART THREE

Belief
in Branding

Harley Davidson's apparent appeal to hardcore bikers creates a brand that, in the reputed words of a Harley marketing executive, enables 'a 43-year-old accountant to dress in black leather, ride through small towns and have people be afraid of him'.

Section 7 – About Courage

There is a fundamental issue here which lies at the heart of any creative activity. Some people believe that through thorough, systematic and careful research, you can arrive at a creative conclusion that will be successful in the marketplace. I don't.

I believe research is useful in telling you what people currently think and feel, but it's not much use at directing the creative process. You get the best results through developing the most creative and original ideas, believing in them and implementing them thoroughly, enthusiastically and rigorously. In my experience the very best, most effective ideas come from inside the heads of creative people. This is true not only in branding, but in any creative activity – the theatre, the cinema, TV – and even advertising. So the answer to the CEO who asks, 'How do you know if it will work?' is 'You have to have the courage of my convictions!' Courage is key.

Sensible research has its place, but it shouldn't be used as a substitute for creative decision-making. It's very important to rely on creative instinct, but it's also necessary to balance the creative instinct with judgment and interpretation.

Researching name and visual style: focus groups

Is it practical to research the whole programme or individual parts of it – names, colours, symbols – before it is launched through focus groups? The argument goes that such research, while it may not tell you what will work, will definitely tell you what won't. I don't agree. Most focus group-based research is, in my experience, not much use. First because a few people paid a little money to sit in a room with others whom they may never have met, discussing a subject about which they know little, are very likely to be cautious and conservative so that they don't appear foolish; second, because most people are initially conservative anyway and don't like anything new.

It is of course essential to go through all the proper procedures to check that any proposed new names are both available and culturally and linguistically acceptable wherever the organization operates. It is also important to understand that certain colours and shapes have specific implications in different parts of the world. Many organizations feel, as I do, that informal discussions with a representative sample of internal and external client contacts worldwide is a helpful and economical way of dealing with this issue.

Researching impact

Most organizations quite reasonably want to know whether their new branding programme has worked. Their questions are: what did I get for what I spent? What did people think of my organization before? What do they think of it now?

So after a programme has been launched, some companies carry out tracking studies to check the extent to which the new branding programme has affected the attitude of different groups of people towards the organization. Research of this kind is well tried and for the most part pretty reliable. It will not tell you what target audiences think of the branding but, much more importantly, what they think of the organization and how their perceptions have changed over time. I recommend it.

Section 8 – Risk

All change involves risk. Branding change inevitably involves some element of risk, too. However, the decision to change or modify branding normally arises because changes in the organization's environment have provoked the organization to reconsider its positioning. The branding change is one of the manifestations of change which the organization has to undertake in order to survive and grow successfully. This is the light in which risks should be regarded.

I have outlined two major risks to the successful implementation of a branding programme at various points in this handbook.

In summary these are:

— First, that the organization creates and launches a branding programme which promises more than it can deliver. Nothing creates more scepticism than an organization which claims to have changed when it hasn't.

— Second, that the organization launches the programme but does not sustain it. Different parts of the organization ignore the new identity, modify it to suit themselves – or even implicitly ridicule it, thereby bringing it into contempt. In this case it is usually perceived by those who come into contact with it as a superficial and cosmetic exercise.

In summary, there is much more risk in handling a brand badly internally than from any external threat.

Section 9 – Brand Valuation

Tangible assets, buildings, plant, machinery have always had a place on the balance sheet. Traditionally intangible assets haven't, although in recent years this has been changing. Intangible assets like intellectual property, in the form of patents, brands and so on, are becoming increasingly valuable.

Over the years a great many sensible companies have paid a great deal of money for brands. So it isn't surprising that accountants and some branding consultancies and other specialists have created complex econometric formulae both to value brands in the short and medium term and to justify a significant place for them in the corporate balance sheet. The idea behind all this is that they fit into the corporate financial accounts in a way that is logical, rational and above all susceptible to numerical analysis. All this is entirely understandable and I am most sympathetic to companies attempting this task, particularly if they happen to be a Coca-Cola or a Virgin, when it is clear the brand is by far their most significant asset.

Unfortunately, though, brand valuation according to these formulae is almost entirely theoretical and has no practical value, because however complex the valuation formula may be, it cannot possibly take into account all the possible eventualities that might affect a brand. Brands may be badly marketed, they may go out of fashion, they may be superseded by a new product or service, the competition may overwhelm them, there may be a quality disaster: the list of 'might happens' is endless. So while I entirely understand why brand valuation is important and why so many people try so hard to undertake it, I'm also clear that the whole process has to be treated with extreme caution.

There's only one reliable way to establish the value of a brand and that is to see what people will pay for it.

Afterword

As I was finalizing this handbook, I started to think back on all the branding programmes I've worked on – what goes wrong, what goes right. Why do some last so long (3i, Repsol, Orange, First Direct)? Why do some fall to bits so quickly? And leaving aside the inevitable fortunes and misfortunes of management – takeovers, mergers, dramatic shifts in technology, and so on – I think the answer is commitment.

I've written about commitment by implication at other points in the handbook when I refer to leadership, to embedding brand management into the company in the same way as IT and financial systems, but I want, as a concluding point, to emphasize again that when the leadership of the company is committed, the systems are in place and the power-base is clear, then, other things being equal, the brand will not just take hold within the organization, it will be seen to be the symbol of what the organization stands for; it will be the force for loyalty, high levels of service and exemplary behaviour towards customers, and it will symbolize the long-term values of the company externally. It will be a treasure beyond price.

So what's the lesson? After the excitement of the launch, don't neglect the brand, or ignore it, or take it for granted. It's a vital part of the corporate DNA. Look after it.

Good luck.

Appendix A
The basic elements

These are the basic elements that make up the visual system of a corporate brand:
— name
— subsidiary names (if appropriate)
— symbol
— main typeface
— subsidiary typefaces (if appropriate)
— colours.
In addition, increasingly, sound and smell are being incorporated into the basic elements vocabulary.

Appendix B
Checklist for the visual audit

This is a standard checklist of product/service items over which the visual elements are usually applied. Experience indicates that the list is appropriate for most companies, but it may need modifying in particular cases.

Products
— product design
— product identification
— rating plates
— operating instructions
— calibration instructions

Packaging
— inners
— outer cartons
— labelling
— delivery instructions
— installation instructions

Environments (interiors/exteriors)
— buildings
— reception areas
— sales areas
— offices
— factories
— shops
— showrooms

Signs
— way-finding
— sign system – internal and external

Exhibitions
— stands, panels
— handouts/giveaways
— passes

Clothing
— badges
— safety hats, overalls, lab coats
— uniforms

Communication materials
— stationery – letter heads, compliment slips, business cards
— meeting notes and agendas
— envelopes
— address labels
— visitor passes
— all marketing communication materials

Digital
— websites
— intranets
— blogs
— screensavers

Promotions
— promotional and point-of-sale materials

Forms
— accounting
— purchasing
— sales
— production
— personnel

Publications
— corporate
— personnel/training
— industry packages
— product

Vehicles
— road transport
— factory transport

Advertising
— corporate
— recruitment
— product/services

Appendix C
Audiences
Internal and quasi-internal audiences
— all staff, at all levels, in all companies and divisions, in all countries
— families of employees
— representatives of trade unions
— shareholders
— directors
— pensioners

External audiences
There are some main external audiences:
— central government, regional government, local government
— competitors
— suppliers
— customers, both direct and indirect
— opinion formers
— journalists
— investment analysts, merchant bankers, stockbrokers
— potential recruits
— schools and universities
— trade and industry associations.

Appendix D
How branding helps

Any branding programme will not succeed by itself in making change. An effective identity underlines change, helps it to happen and continually reminds an organization what its goals are.

The benefits a programme can bring must therefore always be seen as part of a package of improvements.

With this proviso the benefits that a change in brand can bring are as follows:

— It allows the process of change to take place more quickly and easily inside an organization.
— It enables organizations to tell the people with whom they deal what they stand for, what they are, what they do and how they do it. It enables them to explain how their activities relate to each other.
— It encourages tighter and more coherent messages of all kinds to emerge from the corporation.
— It enables people who deal with the company to understand its corporate goals and objectives.

Because of these advantages, a well-organized corporate branding programme also brings other advantages.

Internal
— It can improve morale and motivation.
— It can reduce staff turnover.
— It can enable better products of more consistent quality to be produced.
— It can enable the company to attract a better calibre of employee than its more anonymous competitors.
— It can enable people from different parts of the organization to work together more effectively.

Financial
— It can make for higher recognition in financial circles, and therefore often favourably affects share prices.
— It can allow acquisitions to be made with less difficulty.
— It can allow organizations to defend themselves more effectively against potential predators.

Marketing
— It can encourage consumers to look more favourably upon the company and its products and to stay brand-loyal.
— It can encourage suppliers to operate regularly and consistently.
— It can allow for more cost-effective expenditure in terms of activities and promotion.
— It can enable the company to establish itself more effectively in new markets.
— It can allow for more rapid emergence of new activities within a company.

Acknowledgments

I would like to thank all my colleagues in Saffron both past and present for all their work in developing the brand discipline and in helping to articulate it.

I would like to thank Jeremy Hildreth and Ben Knapp for reading, rereading and finding and checking all my errors, both of omission and commission; Jo Jenkins for examining and developing the project management section; and Claire Fenton for endlessly typing and retyping the draft as it changed and developed.

I would also like to thank Eric Scott and Natasha Chandani for a beautiful and useful piece of design (the book), carried out with great enthusiasm and great speed.

Picture credits

p. 6 Photo by Saffron; p. 7 Flickr/Steve Webel (detail); p. 9 below Photo by Saffron; pp. 10–11 Photo by Alexander Tamargo/Getty Images; p. 12 top Courtesy London 2012; p. 12 centre and below Courtesy Conservative Party, UK; p. 13 above Flickr/Scandblue (detail); p. 13 below Photo by Chung Sung-Jun/Getty Images; pp. 14–15 Courtesy BP UK; p. 17 Photo by Saffron; p. 18 below Flickr/celineki; p. 19 Flickr/phoosh (detail); p. 20 Courtesy Lloyd's of London; p. 21 Courtesy BBC; pp. 22–23 Photo by Cliver Brunskill/Getty Images; p. 25 Courtesy Vueling S.A.; pp. 26–27 Photo by Paul Gilham/Getty Images; p. 28 above Flickr/(RED); p. 28 below M. Spencer Green/AP; p. 29 above Courtesy city of Lille; p. 29 below Courtesy Australian Tourist Board; p. 30 Courtesy Mondragón Industrial Cooperative; pp. 32–33 Courtesy BMW; p. 34 Flickr/smilebrigade (detail); p. 35 Courtesy Hofbräuhaus; pp. 36–37 Flickr/random letters; p. 38 Courtesy Jumeirah Hotels; p. 40 Courtesy Kempinski Hotels; p. 42 above Photo by Mario Tama/Gettyimages; p. 42 below Courtesy Singapore Airlines; p. 43 Photo by Hans Neleman/Gettyimages; p. 46 above Flickr/marirs; p. 46 below Flickr/hyku; p. 47 above Courtesy Harvard University; p. 47 Courtyard Marriott: www.brandsoftheworld.com; p. 47 bottom Courtesy Bankinter S.A.; p. 49 Photo by Mark Wilson/Gettyimages; p. 51 www.business2000.ie; p. 52 above Flickr/crowd_surfer100 (detail); p. 52 below Photos by Jeremy Hildreth; p. 55 above Flickr/digitonin (detail); p. 55 below Courtesy British Telecom; p. 56 above Photo by Saffron; p. 56 below Photo by Jeremy Hildreth; p. 56 Courtesy Accenture; p. 57 Courtesy Shell Group; pp. 58–59 Courtesy FedEx; p. 61 second from top Flickr/philcarrizzi (detail); p. 61 third from top Flickr/Synthesis Studios (detail); p. 61 bottom Flickr/DaveMN (detail); p. 62 above Photo by Ralph Morse/ Gettyimages; p. 62 below Photo by Saffron; pp. 62–63 Photo by Robyn Beck/AFP/Gettyimages; p. 83 Flickr/ superman ha muerto; p. 85 Courtesy IXE Bank, Mexico; p. 86 Courtesy TeliaSonera; p. 87 Courtesy Renault; p. 95 Courtesy Leon; p. 99 Courtesy Lloyd's of London; pp. 100–01 Photo by Rebecca Lewis/Getty Images.

Every effort has been made to locate and credit copyright holders of the material reproduced in this book. The author and publisher apologize for any omissions or errors, which can be corrected in future editions.

Index

Wally
The E
Hand